ENGLISH DR

Series Editor
Bruce King

ENGLISH DRAMATISTS

Series Editor: Bruce King

Published titles

Richard Cave, *Ben Jonson*
Christine Richardson and Jackie Johnston, *Medieval Drama*
Roger Sales, *Christopher Marlowe*
David Thomas, *William Congreve*
Martin White, *Middleton and Tourneur*
Katharine Worth, *Sheridan and Goldsmith*

Forthcoming titles

Susan Bassnett, *Shakespeare: Elizabethan Plays*
John Bull, *Vanbrugh and Farquhar*
Barbara Kachur, *Etherege and Wycherley*
Phillip McGuire, *Shakespeare: Jacobean Plays*
Kate McLuskie, *Dekker and Heywood*
Maximillian Novak, *Fielding and Gay*
Cheryl Turner, *Early Women Dramatists*
Rowland Wymer, *Webster and Ford*

ENGLISH DRAMATISTS

WILLIAM CONGREVE

David Thomas

MACMILLAN

First published 1992 by
THE MACMILLAN PRESS LTD
Houndmills, Basingstoke, Hampshire RG21 2XS
and London
Companies and representatives
throughout the world

ISBN 0-333-45478-2 hardcover
ISBN 0-333-45479-0 paperback

A catalogue record for this book is available
from the British Library

Copy-edited and typeset by Povey–Edmondson
Okehampton and Rochdale, England

Printed in Hong Kong

For my mother

Contents

Editor's Preface

Each generation needs to be introduced to the culture and great works of the past and to reinterpret them in its own ways. This series re-examines the important English dramatists of earlier centuries in the light of new information, new interests and new attitudes. The books are written for students, theatre-goers and general readers who want an up-to-date view of the plays and dramatists, with emphasis on drama as theatre and on stage, social and political history. Attention is given to what is known about performance, acting styles, changing interpretations, the stages and theatres of the time and theatre economics. The books will be relevant to those interested in or studying literature, theatre and cultural history.

BRUCE KING

Acknowledgements

During the writing of this book, I have drawn extensively on research I undertook during the 1980s when preparing a reference work on Restoration theatre for Cambridge University Press: *Theatre in Europe: A Documentary History. Restoration and Georgian England, 1660–1780* (1989). For the most part, my book is based on insights gained during my years of university teaching experience, first at Bristol and latterly at Warwick. Both undergraduate and postgraduate students have played their part in sharpening my responses to Congreve, and I would like to express my warmest thanks to all those students who have shared my enthusiasm for his work.

To my former colleagues in the Department of Drama at the University of Bristol I am grateful for giving me, during the 1970s and early 1980s, the opportunity and the resources to mount a series of workshop performances at the Glynne Wickham Studio in Bristol in which scenes from Congreve (as well as other Restoration playwrights) were presented in a reconstruction of a Restoration playhouse (including full candle lighting). These experimental performances confirmed my admiration for Congreve as an essentially theatrical writer.

I am most grateful to John Copley, formerly house producer at Covent Garden, for inviting me to advise him on Congreve's libretto in preparation for his production of *Semele* at the Royal Opera House in 1982. This experience helped me to arrive at a full appreciation of Congreve's skill in the difficult and demanding art of libretto writing.

To the staff of various libraries I am indebted for their courtesy and helpfulness during my research for this volume, in particular to the staff (especially to the keepers of rare books) at the University Libraries of Bristol and Warwick and to the staff in the Reading Room of the British Museum.

I have discussed my ideas for this volume and shared my enthusiasm for Congreve's work not only with colleagues but also with friends and family. One debt of gratitude in this respect (as in many others) I have acknowledged in my dedication. But at this point I would also like to thank Coucou Lyall for her patient and untiring willingness to respond warmly and generously to my latest thoughts and perceptions.

I would like to express my thanks to a number of friends in the town of Warwick for their interest in the progress of my book. Their various life stories (told over a meal or a pint in Warwick's historic Zetland Arms) have convinced me that the inspiration for Congreve's characters was derived, not only from the players he knew at Lincoln's Inn Fields, but above all from the stories he listened to at Will's and White's. Even the political debate in which Congreve so passionately engaged in the 1690s still echoes in the inns and drawing-rooms of England during the 1990s and is part of the fabric of our modern lives.

The technological wonders of an IBM PS/2 and a Toshiba portable (along with the latest version of Wordstar) have made the process of writing this book a real pleasure. It was written during the course of three glorious summers which, thanks to the Toshiba, could be fully savoured on a sunny terrace in the Queen Anne and Georgian splendours of the town of Warwick. A much-needed period of study leave during the summer of 1991 (for which I am most grateful to the University of Warwick) enabled me to complete the volume without the myriad pressures confronting a senior academic in a thriving modern university.

Turning now to the work of critics and editors who have contributed significantly to a new understanding of Congreve, I would like to record my appreciation of Montague Summers's pioneering work in the early 1920s in preparing the first complete edition of Congreve's work, based on the acting quartos of the plays and the first editions of other works. It is still the only such complete edition of Congreve's work available and I have therefore used it as the basis for my quotations from Congreve's plays, poems and prose works. A reference in square brackets immediately following a quotation gives the appropriate volume number and page in the Summers edition.

Finally, my personal debt to other scholars and critics who have written on Congreve is freely acknowledged in both text and notes. My book offers new insights into Congreve's work, based on a firm understanding of the political and theatrical context in which he was working, but it also owes a great deal to the many who have already wrestled with the complexities and responded to the beauties of Congreve's work.

Castle Lane, Warwick DAVID THOMAS

List of Plates

Reproduced from the author's collection

1
Life and Work

Congreve the man is an elusive figure. Throughout his life he seemed content to remain at the edges of fame and fortune. Time and again he showed himself loath to advance his own case with totally committed energy and instead preferred to withdraw to the isolation and sanctuary of his study. He was passionately involved in the political issues of his age but never directly in political action. He was committed to extending the frontiers of comic writing in the theatre and yet preferred to withdraw from the theatre altogether rather than suffer the indignity of public misunderstanding and rejection. He was a passionate lover and yet never managed to find a mistress to whom he could commit himself without having to resort to constant deception and subterfuge. His whole life seemed an urbane and studied attempt to transform life's inevitable vicissitudes and disappointments, through a series of deliberately planned rational strategies, into a harmonious and pleasing pattern.

This philosophical approach to life (which has some similarities to the Nietzschean view that it is only as an aesthetic phenomenon that life is justified) goes a long way towards explaining why Congreve the man seems such an anonymous figure. The rough edges of experience have been deliberately smoothed away; very little of his innermost feelings are revealed to the world; and any powerful appetites, in particular his sexual appetite, have been tamed or at least carefully channelled in such a way as to preserve

1

his social poise and decorum. Congreve deliberately covered his tracks so that it is as difficult to come to a definite conclusion about his behaviour and attitudes as it is when confronted by one of the complex and subtle figures drawn by Ibsen or Chekhov. Because of this, his reputation has suffered greatly at the hands of eighteenth- and nineteenth-century critics and biographers. Dr Johnson, for instance, criticised Congreve for his supposed failure to acknowledge Ireland as the place of his birth.[1] Other critics have too readily accepted Voltaire's dismissive view of Congreve as vain and foolish because he had stated to the presumptuous young author that he wished to be visited 'upon no other Foot than that of a Gentleman'.[2] His relationship with Anne Bracegirdle has often been viewed as essentially patronising and exploitative. In addition, there has been general puzzlement at his will in which he left most of his estate to Henrietta, Duchess of Marlborough, who was already one of the richest women in Europe, while seemingly treating both Anne Bracegirdle and his family with comparative neglect.[3] Given the thoroughness with which Congreve hid the details of his personal life from his contemporaries, such misunderstandings are only to be expected. In contrast, the testimony of friends and fellow-writers suggests that Congreve was a man of great kindness and sensitivity, whose judgement was highly valued and whose company was esteemed. It is also clear from the evidence of his correspondence that he remained passionately loyal to his few chosen friends throughout his life.[4]

Congreve was born in Bardsey, Yorkshire, on 24 January 1670. His father, William Congreve, was the second son of a Staffordshire squire who had suffered considerable financial embarrassment as a result of his royalist commitment during the civil war. In the late 1660s, William had married Mary Browning who was related to the wealthy Lewis family of Yorkshire. At the time of Congreve's birth his parents were living at Bardsey Grange on part of Sir John Lewis's family estate. Four years later, following a long family tradition, Congreve's father joined the army and moved to Ireland. He was given a commission as a lieutenant in the Irish army and travelled with his family to the garrison at the port of Youghal. In 1678 the family moved to Carrickfergus and then in 1681 to Kilkenny where Congreve's father joined the Duke of Ormond's regiment. This permitted Congreve to have free education in the splendid school, Kilkenny College, endowed by the Duke of Ormond. For a brief period, his schooling at Kilkenny overlapped that of Jonathan Swift, but it is unlikely that they had any contact with each other at the time. However, Congreve made one close friend at Kilkenny, Joseph Keally, with whom he was to remain in contact throughout his adult life. Apart from a good general education, Kilkenny College gave Congreve a secure grounding in classical language and literature, which was later to stand him in good stead as a member of Dryden's literary circle.

Congreve left Kilkenny in 1686 to continue his studies at Trinity College, Dublin. He was not a particularly assiduous scholar, and the College was in any case faced with growing difficulties because of the accession to the throne of the Catholic King James II. Congreve used his time in Dublin to strengthen his command of the classics as well as an opportunity to acquaint himself with the theatre and the delights of good food and wine. Because of political pressures, the College was obliged to close in 1689 for a span and Congreve decided to move to England. By 1691 his father could afford to enrol him as a law student in the Middle Temple but Congreve seemingly paid scant attention to legal studies. Instead he dedicated himself with some enthusiasm to the pursuit of a literary career, joining the circle of wits and writers who gathered at Will's Coffee House. In particular, he became a close friend of Dryden, who was by then the grand old man of English letters, and contributed a translation of some fragments from Homer to Dryden's *Examen Poeticum* of 1693. Dryden was fulsome in his praise of Congreve's talents as a translator: in the dedication of his volume to Edward, Lord Radclyffe, he wrote:

Notwithstanding my haste, I cannot forbear to tell your Lordship, that there are two fragments of *Homer* Translated in this *Miscellany*; one by Mr *Congreve* (whom I cannot mention without the Honour which is due to his excellent Parts, and that entire Affection which I bear him;) and the other by my self. Both the Subjects are pathetical; and I am sure my Friend has added to the Tenderness which he found in the Original; and, without Flattery, surpass'd his Author.[5]

In 1691 Congreve published a short novel called *Incognita* which he had written in Trinity College some years previously.

However, the tentative nature of this undertaking was under-scored by the fact that Congreve decided to publish the work anonymously. The following year, 1692, brought a major development in his literary career. While on a visit to Ilam in Dovedale, he finished working on the text of a play called *The Old Batchelour* and submitted it to Dryden for advice. Dryden declared that it was one of the best first plays he had ever seen, although he proposed a number of alterations and amendments to suit it to 'the fashionable cutt of the town'.[6] In its revised form, Thomas Southerne, a friend and fellow-writer, commended the manuscript to Thomas Davenant, then manager of the Theatre Royal, Drury Lane. The play was accepted for performance in late 1692, but because of problems associated with changes in the acting company, it was not finally performed until March 1693. It was an enormous success and brought Congreve fame almost overnight.

While waiting for his play to be performed, Congreve had ample time to observe the Drury Lane company in rehearsal. It was almost certainly at this period that he began to fall in love with the actress, Anne Bracegirdle, who was playing the role of Araminta in *The Old Batchelour*. When Congreve began working on his next play *The Double Dealer* he wrote the role of Cynthia, the virtuous heroine, for Anne Bracegirdle whose lover Mellefont in the play seems to plead Congreve's own cause.[7] The play was performed in December 1693 and was generally disliked. Congreve's closest friends and colleagues, Dryden notable among them, gave him and his play unqualified support, but Congreve was deeply upset. In the first edition of the play, he directed a ferocious attack against his play's critics.[8] Wisely he omitted his attack from later editions of the play. The episode demonstrates, however, something of the sensibility that was to lead him within a few years to quit writing for the stage altogether.

His next play *Love for Love* was written in 1694. Again there was a major role for Anne Bracegirdle who was to play the witty and resourceful heroine, Angelica. However, dissension in the theatre company at Drury Lane meant an unavoidable delay in bringing the play to performance. Congreve supported the leading actors in the company in their revolt against the manager, Christopher Rich, and in their attempt to persuade the Lord

Chamberlain to grant them a licence to form their own theatre company at Lincoln's Inn Fields. Their petition succeeded and the actors' company opened their newly converted theatre with a triumphant production of *Love for Love* in 1695. As a result Congreve was himself made a shareholder in the company. 1695 was a good year for Congreve. Apart from the success he enjoyed with *Love for Love*, his reputation as a poet was at its zenith. In December 1694 he had written a pastoral poem entitled *The Mourning Muse of Alexis* which lamented 'the death of our late gracious Queen Mary'. This was widely regarded by his contemporaries as one of his finest literary achievements. That same year he was rewarded for his loyalty to the Whig cause in politics with his first political appointment: he was made a Commissioner for Hackney coaches at the modest fee of £100 p.a. In making this appointment, William III's ministers doubtless hoped that Congreve would use his considerable literary talents in the Whig cause and they were not disappointed. Within a matter of months, Congreve published his *Pindarique Ode humbly offer'd to the King, on his taking Namure*, which was full of the most extravagant praise of King William's epic martial exploits.

In the summer months of 1695, he was engaged in a correspondence with the critic, John Dennis. One of his letters to Dennis, arising from this correspondence, was in effect an urbane and polished essay on the topic of 'Humour in Comedy'. Other letters gave an amusing account of his own stay during the summer at the spa town of Tunbridge Wells, where the assembled company appeared to have the 'Appetite of an Oastrich'.[9] Congreve's health had begun to give him trouble, hence his regular visit to spa towns to take the waters. His excessive fondness of a good meal and a good bottle had brought him problems of overweight, dyspepsia and gout. His gout was to become progressively worse over the years to come.

In 1696 it seems likely that he visited his parents in Ireland.[10] His father had recently retired from the army with the rank of colonel and had been appointed agent of the Earl of Cork and Burlington at his castle at Lismore. It seems likely that it was during this visit that Congreve wrote or at least began work on his first tragedy, *The Mourning Bride*. The play was performed at Lincoln's Inn Fields in February 1697 and was another outstanding success.

In many ways this production marked the pinnacle of his career. The following year, 1698, brought an unpleasant setback in the shape of the Jeremy Collier controversy. Collier was a nonjuring High Church clergyman with a taste for social and political disputes. His political opposition to the Protestant monarch, King William III, had threatened to land him in prison. Prudently, he turned his attention to less dangerous material and wrote a vituperative critique of the contemporary stage in 1698 called *A Short View of the Immorality and Profaneness of the English Stage: Together with the Sense of Antiquity upon this Argument*. Most unwisely, a number of playwrights, including Vanbrugh and Congreve, were provoked into publishing a series of replies to this swingeing critique. Congreve's was entitled *Amendments of Mr Collier's False and Imperfect Citations* and was a misplaced attempt to use rational arguments in an essentially irrational debate. Congreve was badly shaken by this episode, and in particular by the realisation that Collier's hostile view of the stage commanded widespread support.

In 1699 Congreve began working on his comic masterpiece *The Way of the World*, which was given its first performance on 12 March 1700. It contained yet another demanding role for Anne Bracegirdle as the delightful and yet mercurial Millamant who resists committing herself to Mirabell until the very last. There was much of Congreve in the bemused figure of Mirabell attempting to fathom out the shifts of mood and wit in his whimsical mistress. But there was one difference. On stage, Anne, in the character of Millamant, was brought to the point of finally agreeing to marry her suitor. In reality, that moment never came. Nor did the triumph the play merited. Congreve knew that he had surpassed himself in this work. But it was too subtle and too complex for the current taste of the town, as Congreve himself acknowledged in his dedication of the play to Ralph, Earl of Montague: 'little of it was prepar'd for that general Taste which seems now to be predominant in the Pallats of our Audience' [Summer edn, vol. 3, p. 9]. He expressed surprise that it had succeeded on the stage; in reality, however, it had enjoyed only a modest success. Unwilling to compromise his approach to playwriting, Congreve resolved to cease writing plays altogether.

This did not mean, however, an immediate and total break with the stage. In the very same year, Congreve was commissioned to write the text of a masque, *The Judgement of Paris*, to form the basis for an exciting operatic competition. A group of wealthy sponsors, headed by Lord Halifax and including the Duke of Somerset, placed an advertisement in the *London Gazette* for 18 March 1700, announcing that they would be offering four prizes in a competition for the encouragement of music 'to such Masters as shall be adjudged to compose the best' and inviting 'those who intend to put in for Prizes . . . to repair to Jacob Tonson at Grays-Inn-Gate'. Four composers entered the competition and each was given the task of writing a musical setting for Congreve's masque. The resulting works were each given a separate performance at Dorset Garden and then all four were performed together on 3 June 1701 to allow the audience of subscribers to vote on which version pleased the most. The winner was an outsider, John Weldon, organist at New College, Oxford. His setting was a splendidly melodic version which greatly pleased the wealthy connoisseurs who had subscribed to the series.[11] However, the setting that enjoyed the most widespread popularity at the time was that of John Eccles, although it was voted second in the actual competition.[12] Eccles was at the time not only Master of the King's Musicians but also the house composer at Lincoln's Inn Fields. It was his version that was performed first on 21 March 1701. In a letter to his friend, Joseph Keally, Congreve wrote enthusiastically about this opening performance and in particular about the way Anne Bracegirdle as Venus had 'performed to a miracle'.[13]

Over the next few years, Congreve was involved with Vanbrugh in the planning of a new theatre and opera house in the Haymarket. Vanbrugh designed the building and the two men raised the building capital by organising a subscription of twenty-nine persons of quality who each paid a share of 100 guineas. In 1705 Vanbrugh and Congreve were given a licence for their new theatre in the Haymarket by Queen Anne (ironically on the grounds that Her Majesty 'thought fit for the reforming the abuses and immorality of the stage').[14] It seems likely that Vanbrugh intended to open the new theatre with an opera production, given his own interest in opera and the current success enjoyed by Drury Lane with its production of Thomas Clayton's *Arsinoe, Queen of Cyprus*. However, as late as February 1705 Congreve wrote to Joseph Keally: 'I know not when the house will open, nor what we shall begin withal; but I believe with no opera. There is nothing settled yet.'[15] This cryptic comment conceals more than it reveals. Following the success of *The Judgement of Paris* and his *Ode for St Cecilia's Day* (1701), which John Eccles had set to music, Congreve had almost certainly been working on an opera libretto with a view to its performance at the opening of the Queen's Theatre in the Haymarket. Given his previous happy experience of working with John Eccles, it was only natural that Congreve should ask Eccles to provide the musical score for his opera, *Semele*. Unfortunately, it would seem that Eccles was by then more interested in fishing than in composing and was unable to complete the libretto in time for the opening of the theatre.[16] Much to Congreve's chagrin, the new theatre had to open on 9 April 1705 with a production of an Italian pastoral opera, Jakob Greber's *The Loves of Ergasto*, the first opera to be sung completely in Italian on the London stage. It proved to be an expensive failure. Congreve himself could not resist composing a snide epilogue for this opening production:

> To Sound and Show at first we make Pretence,
> In Time we may regale you with some Sense,
> But that, at present, were too great Expence.[17]

Worse was to follow. The playhouse proved to be a commercial liability. Not only was it built in the wrong part of town (at the time none of the elegant squares had been built that later came to adjoin the Haymarket), but it appeared to have serious design flaws. Colley Cibber, for instance, draws attention to problems of acoustics,[18] but there were also difficulties in respect of sight lines.[19] By December 1705, the prospect of substantial losses seemed unavoidable. Congreve decided to buy his way out, while he still could. As he commented in a letter to his friend, Joseph Keally: 'I have nothing to add but only that I have quitted the affair of the Hay-market. You may imagine I got nothing by it . . . '.[20]

As a sad postscript to Congreve's involvement with the Haymarket, it is worth noting that Eccles's score for *Semele* was ready for performance by 1707. During that season, the theatrical arch-rival of Congreve and Vanbrugh, Christopher Rich, had been given a monopoly over opera productions in London. Congreve's libretto, set to music by Eccles, was therefore offered to Rich and was reported by *The Muses Mercury*, a monthly journal devoted to the arts, to be 'ready to be practised' in January 1707.[21] However, it was never performed and probably never even rehearsed as Rich mounted a highly successful production of an Italian opera called *Thomyris* in April 1707 which played for a lengthy run. This final disappointment marked Congreve's real break with the theatre.

This break mirrored events in Congreve's personal life, notably a change in his relationship with Anne Bracegirdle. Since the mid-1690s, they had been neighbours, living in adjoining streets just off the Strand. According to at least one contemporary report, they had ridden and dined with each other almost every day.[22] Although they were too discreet for the town to be certain about the exact nature of their relationship, their daily contact suggests very strongly that they were lovers. However, around 1702 to 1703, Congreve's cousin, Robert Leke, third Earl of Scarsdale, began to show a strong interest in Anne to which she seemingly responded. (Leke even specified a handsome bequest to her in a will he drew up on 9 January 1703.) Congreve set down his feelings in verse form:

> In hours of bliss we oft have met,
> They could not allways last;
> And tho' the present I regret,
> I still am Gratefull for the past [. . .]
> Who may your future favours own
> May future change forgive;
> In Love, the first deceit alone
> Is what you never can retrieve.[23]

He remained on amicable terms with his neighbour (and in his turn left her a small bequest of £200 in his will), but their relationship would never again blossom with the same intensity as it had since the early 1690s.

Congreve's life for the next five years was very much that of a loner. He suffered from gout and cataracts in his eyes that threatened him with blindness. He obtained a new political post with effect from 1705 when he became Commissioner for Wines at an annual salary of £200. He wrote occasional poems, but no longer produced any work for the theatre. In 1710 he prepared a collected edition of his work. His one relaxation appears to have centred on meetings of the Kit-Cat Club, a group of distinguished writers and Whig politicians who gathered at the house of the publisher, Jacob Tonson.

Congreve's company was valued by writers such as Swift and Pope, but one cannot help noticing in their written comments some sense of pity for a man whose ill-health and lack of preferment have reduced him to almost straitened circumstances:

> Congreve scarce could spare
> A shilling to discharge his chair.[24]

Luckily, Swift made pleas on Congreve's behalf to the Lord Treasurer, Robert Harley, during the Tory administration of 1710 to 1714, which permitted him to retain his minor post as Commissioner for Wines.

A noticeable change for the better in Congreve's fortunes occurred with the accession of George I in 1714 and the establishing of a firm Whig government. At long last, his powerful friends procured for him a reasonably well-paid government sinecure. He was made Secretary to the Island of Jamaica at an annual salary of £700. Despite this trebling of his income, Congreve continued to live simply in his humble lodgings with Edward and Frances Porter in Surrey Street near the Strand.[25]

Another important change in Congreve's life occurred around the same period. A social relationship between himself and Lady Henrietta Godolphin blossomed into a love affair lasting for the remainder of his life. Henrietta had married Francis Godolphin (later Earl of Godolphin) in 1698. She was the eldest daughter of the Duke and Duchess of Marlborough and, at her father's death in 1722, the title of Duchess of Marlborough was conferred on her by special grant of Parliament. It is not known for certain when she and Congreve first met.

Congreve had written poetical tributes to Henrietta's brother who died in 1703 and to her father-in-law, Sidney Godolphin, in 1706.[26] Whether this led to any immediate social contact is not known. What is clear is that by 1714 the two were firm friends.

Their friendship was heartily disapproved of by Henrietta's termagant mother, Sarah, Duchess of Marlborough who commented, 'She soon fell into very ill company, My Lady Oxford & Her daughters, Mrs Ramsey & Mrs Hamond, Afterwards my Lady Sandwich, & at last having a great mind to be thought a Wit Mr Congreve & several Poets, and in short the worst company that a Young Lady can keep.'[27] On one occasion, she apparently found them playing at ombre with another woman and claimed that Congreve, 'look'd out of Countenance'.[28] The two of them gradually became inseparable. Their discretion was such that their contact was tolerated by Francis Godolphin, Henrietta's husband, and generally accepted by their contemporaries.

It is not difficult to see the reasons for their mutual attraction. Congreve was a far-from-wealthy man who was not in the best of health. To be idolised and cosseted by a beautiful young aristocratic woman must have seemed a not unattractive proposition. For her part, Henrietta, who was at loggerheads with an emotionally demanding mother and frankly bored with a kind but uninspiring husband, must have been flattered and excited by the attention of a man who was acknowledged as one of the greatest wits and writers of the age.

One likely consequence of their relationship, after a season spent together in Bath, was the birth in November 1723 of a daughter, christened Mary. Another consequence was a certain frustration felt by Congreve's friends, notably Pope, that he now spent so much time with Henrietta that there was precious little left for them.[29]

For Congreve his relationship with Henrietta brought a sense of stability and meaning to what had so often seemed a world absurdly out of joint. Henrietta proved a loyal and devoted companion, who gladly shared her time with him, loving him and cherishing him in sickness and in health. In 1726, for instance, she tended him at her home, Windsor Lodge, for several weeks while he lay ill of 'a fever and the gout in his stomach'.[30] In 1728, Congreve's health was again very poor and he remained at Bath with Henrietta from May to October. In that same year he wrote a valedictory Horatian Epistle to his friend Lord Cobham. He died at his Surrey Street lodgings on 19 January 1729. Henrietta was with him to the last and kept vigil by his coffin all night long. She ensured, not only that he was properly buried in Westminster Abbey, but that she herself would lie close to him after her own death in 1733. Theirs was a love match that seemed to last beyond the grave.

Congreve's final stratagem for imposing a sense of rational order on life's absurdities was the will he drew up in favour of Henrietta. By making her husband, Francis Godolphin, the executor, he cut away all possibility of gossip. But by bequeathing his estate directly to her, and directing that, 'her said Husband or any after taken Husband of her the said Dutchess of Marlborough shall not intermeddle or have any controuling power over' the estate,[31] he ensured that only she could have access to the money. The purpose that had obviously been agreed by them both was that Henrietta should buy a set of diamonds to bequeath to her youngest daughter. On the back of every collet would be carved the poet's initials.[32] In this way, Henrietta's daughter would inherit from the man who was almost certainly her natural father a gift of rare beauty, worthy of a man and a lover whose brilliant wit had once charmed the whole of London.

The final image Congreve left of himself may be found in the closing verses of his *Epistle to Lord Cobham*, published after Congreve's death in 1729. They reveal a great deal about the man who strove to forget his many cares and to face life's absurdities and cruel ironies with studied equanimity. Their sense of deliberately sustained poise and decorum in the face of the 'World's new wicked Ways' (a pointed reference to his earlier play) provide a fitting epitaph for a man who, while conscious of the potential absurdity of existence, chose to live out his life as if it were a rationally conceived work of art:

> Come, see thy Friend, retir'd without Regret,
> Forgetting Care, or striving to forget;
> In easy Contemplation soothing Time
> With Morals much, and now and then with Rhime,
> Not so robust in Body, as in Mind,
> And always undejected, tho' declin'd;
> Not wondering at the World's new wicked Ways,
> Compar'd with those of our Fore-fathers Days,
> For Virtue now is neither more or less,

And Vice is only varied in the Dress;
Believe it, Men have ever been the same,
And all the Golden Age, is but a Dream.[33]

2
The Literary Context

At the end of Etherege's play *The Man of Mode* (1676), the audience is left with a question in its mind. The major characters, Harriet and Dorimant have declared in asides to the audience the strength of their feelings for each other but they do not trust each other and cannot find the right vocabulary to talk directly to each other. The question is: will they ever find sufficient trust, in London or the country, on which to base a viable relationship?

In *The Way of the World* (1700), even before the action begins, the leading characters Millamant and Mirabell have effectively decided to commit themselves to each other. In their case, what is at stake is not the possibility of commitment, but rather the detailed structuring of their relationship together. Most of the play traces out their attempts to ensure that they will have sufficient property to sustain them in some comfort; while the provisos they run through in Act 4 are intended to furnish in effect a contractual base for their daily lives together, ensuring a considerable degree of personal independence within an overall framework of mutual commitment.

Writing in 1700, Congreve is able to begin his play, in human and emotional terms, at a point well beyond the stage of ambiguity which Etherege reached at the conclusion of *The Man of Mode*. This essential difference between the two plays illustrates a substantial shift in the temper of English society between the mid-1670s and the turn of the century: a shift from the scepticism of the Restoration with its post-civil-war mistrust of emotion and commitment, to the ordered constitutionalism of the eighteenth century with its self-confident belief in the ideals of Whig liberalism.

However, Congreve was not a naive Whig apologist, intent on writing the kind of sentimental comedies that were later to become so popular on the eighteenth century stage. His view of life and his approach to playwriting owe much to the traditions of the Restoration. Arguably what makes his work unique is the subtle balance he achieves in it between the cool disenchantment of the Restoration and the emotional warmth of the eighteenth century.

In the Restoration, following the emotional excesses of the civil-war period, there was a general wariness in respect of feeling and an emphasis instead on form. In aesthetic theory, Hobbes had already stressed the primacy of form in his *Answer to Davenant's Preface to Gondibert* (1650): 'Judgement begets the strength and structure, and Fancy begets the ornaments of a Poem.'[1] While judgement or reason is seen as providing the structural strength of a poem, fancy or imagination is merely responsible for the ornamentation or embellishment. It is the shape that matters and the shape is determined by judgement.

Dryden was to echo this same view some years later in his essay *Of Dramatic Poesy* (1668):

> Judgement is indeed the master-workman in a play; but he requires many subordinate hands, many tools to his assistance. And verse I affirm to be one of these; 'tis a rule and line by which he keeps his building compact and even, which otherwise lawless imagination would raise either irregularly or loosely.[2]

What is implied by such a view is that the pattern is everything, a pattern created by the application of sound judgement to the creative process. The imagination is to be mistrusted and is in any case only responsible for style or imagery, which are seen as mere embellishments. It is this that explains the formal quality of Restoration writing, the architectural design of the plays. Tragedy, devoid of genuine emotion and with the imagination held in check, becomes a complex mannerism tending towards the operatic. Comedy, equally formal in terms of structure and characterisation, faithfully reflects the contemporary flight from emotional warmth and commitment. In both cases, it is not *what* the playwright does that matters but *how* he or she does it. The design is everything. As Dryden expressed it in his essay:

> If then the parts are managed so regularly that the beauty of the whole be kept entire, and that the variety become not a perplexed and confused mass of accidents, you will find it infinitely pleasing to be led in a labyrinth of design.[3]

Congreve shares with Restoration playwrights a commitment to judgement and reason as the essential tools in the creative process. His plays are carefully sculpted artifacts in which the author takes a Drydenesque delight in leading the reader or viewer through a labyrinthine plot of some subtlety, but the various constituent parts are indeed 'managed so regularly' that the complexity is always a source of theatrical delight. As one would expect, the major characters in his plays, such as Valentine in *Love for Love* or Mirabell in *The Way of the World*, are inveterate plotters who take great pleasure in attempting to impose their rational strategies for survival on a fickle and fast-changing world. In some of the deceptions and subterfuges, there are echoes from earlier Restoration comedy, but the tone has changed. Congreve's heroes, for the most part, are not merely a bundle of appetites in motion, as is the case in some of the earlier plays; in particular in his last two comedies, they are discreet and civilised individuals who have learnt the art of channelling their appetites into socially acceptable forms. What Congreve does in these late plays is to take the themes and conventions of earlier Restoration writing, smooth off the rough edges of language and behaviour, and probe more analytically into the motives for human interaction and into the relationship between man and society. In his reworking of the themes of Restoration comedy, he transforms them into something distinctively and uniquely his own. If there is one feature that predominates above all others in his late comedies, it is the rational restraint with which he and his major figures respond to the challenges of life.

Restoration comedy took shape as a genre in the 1660s. Based on the comic traditions of Jacobean and Caroline drama, which gave it an earthy grounding, Restoration comedy acquired its elegance and polish from French influences, notably Molière. Sir George Etherege played a crucial role in establishing Restoration comedy as a genre with his two first plays *Love in a Tub* (1664) and *She wou'd if she cou'd* (1668). In both cases, influences from English and French comic traditions are subtly blended together in a gentle mixture of intrigue and wry observation. Scenes reminiscent of Beaumont and Fletcher are linked together in a dance-like rhythm reminiscent of Molière. It was Dryden, in his comedy *The Wild Gallant* (1663), who added what was to be one of the main distinguishing features of Restoration comedy, namely the use of an amoral and sexually hyperactive hero as the main focus of attention. This was an archetype that other writers were swift to exploit.

Probably the best-known of these phallic heroes is Horner in Wycherley's play *The Country Wife* (1675). As his name implies, Horner is a dedicated stud whose main aim in life is to notch up a significant tally of sexual conquests. In order to have access to society women, Horner spreads the false report that he is a harmless eunuch, castrated accidentally by a French surgeon who was trying to cure him of the clap. This makes him, in the eyes of the husbands, an ideal and harmless chaperone for their wives. Using a loose, kaleidoscopic structure, the play then traces out at length his various escapades with the women of the town who show themselves only too willing to satisfy their sexual urges providing their reputations are safe.

Wycherley's approach in the play is self-evidently satiric. What is less clear-cut is the object of his satire. If his concern is primarily with the satiric treatment of individual characters, then the play can seem very ambiguous indeed. Is Horner, for instance, to be criticised or admired? And what of the society women: are they to be seen as pathetic victims or grotesque accomplices of his lust? The resolution of these uncertainties may be found if the play is viewed as a satiric treatment of social convention rather than a satiric view of individual characters. What Wycherley is concerned with in *The Country Wife* is the way social conventions twist human behaviour into foolish and hypocritical patterns. As he sees it, there is an irreconcilable clash between natural instinct and social convention. Above all, there is a clash between human sexual appetite and the socially accepted conventions for channelling sexual behaviour. In Wycherley's eyes, the sexual urge is both a natural and a highly desirable instinct. But it is one that is thwarted in the loveless, arranged marriages of the age. Inevitably, men and women find a way round the problem.

Wycherley recognises that women have the same sexual appetites as men, but because of the double standards of the age and the high esteem placed upon female chastity (a sign of women's complete submission to men), it was essential for women to preserve their reputation and their honour. This placed them in a hypocritical position in society, which is satirised by Wycherley. Repeatedly, he contrasts their natural sexual urges with the behaviour expected of them. Only when alone with Horner, the outsider, can they afford to drop their masks and revel in their sexuality. As Lady Fidget expresses it gleefully in Act 4, 'Let him come, and welcome, which way he will.' For most of the play, their enjoyment is secretive and individual, but in a wild drinking scene in Act 5 they discover that they have all been pleasured by Horner and can now even afford to drop their masks to each other. The contrast between the polite exterior they are normally expected to show the world and the Bacchic disorder into which they joyfully sink with Horner is a telling commentary on their world.

Horner is shown as having many attractive sides to his personality. He is clearly pleasing to the opposite sex and takes delight in celebrating his sexuality. But because of the tightly controlled social conventions of the age, he can only find spontaneous sexual experience by subverting the prohibitions of patriarchal society. There is both a sadness and a loneliness in his having to pretend to be a eunuch in order to find a satisfactory outlet for his sexual desires. Wycherley is aware of this and shows it, but he is himself too much a part of his society to be able to envisage any way of reconciling sexuality, emotion and marital commitment.

The Country Wife is a hard-hitting satire which seriously questions the wisdom or even the possibility of successfully attempting to restrict powerful and natural instincts within conventional fetters. It offers no easy answers. Instead it is structured in such a way as to underline the stalemate achieved at the end. The characters, like the audience watching the play, are locked in stereotyped roles from which they cannot escape. The satiric provocation to the audience is deliberate.

Etherege, in *The Man of Mode* (1676), shows us another variant of the wild gallant in the figure of Dorimant. His approach, however, is less satiric than Wycherley's. Known to his friends as 'Gentle George', Etherege was more tolerant than Wycherley of the men and women he saw around him in Restoration England. In *The Man of Mode* he shows us a group of individuals whose insecurity and fear of exposure, of being given over to scorn and mockery, leads them to construct elaborate poses behind which they conceal their real feelings. Even the way they dress is a deliberate act of subterfuge in which masks and cravats, patches and fans, all play their part in keeping real experience at a safe distance, which is why scenes of dressing and comments on fashion play such an important role in the action.

The play is structured around a series of erotic games, some played in earnest, others half-jestingly. Most revolve around the central figure, Dorimant. Others are played out by minor figures in a variety of briefly sketched-in subplots: the urgent and desperately serious courtship rituals of the young lovers, Emilia and Young Bellair; the foolish lusting of Old Bellair for Emilia; the gentle flirtation of old Lady Woodville with Mr Courtage (Dorimant in disguise). All these various games and intrigues contribute to the overall momentum of the play in an almost dance-like rhythm, the kind of dance in which partners are changed in an elegant but predictable sequence. Some of the games, however, are exceedingly cruel. In particular Dorimant, the main character, executes some exquisitely fiendish strategies for ridding himself of Mrs Loveit, a former mistress whose company he can no longer tolerate. When confronted by her, he does his best to mystify her, at one moment telling her the complete truth, admitting to her face that he is a liar and a cheat, but at the very next moment pretending to be jealous of her for her supposed kindness to a fatuous rival, Sir Fopling Flutter. Eventually Dorimant succeeds in driving Loveit into a state of complete distraction. Throughout this episode, his behaviour is cruel, callous and thoroughly unsympathetic. And yet Loveit, for all her genuine feelings, seems to enjoy playing the role of a tragic heroine, rejected by a tyrannic lover. There is an almost sado-masochistic complementarity in their interaction which is both irrational and yet has the ring of truth about it. Etherege's view of human nature is far too subtle and complex to permit him to use the kind of broad satiric techniques of Wycherley.

The one thing Etherege's characters view with alarm is the possibility that someone may strip away their mask and reveal their true feelings underneath. This is precisely what happens to Loveit, and it is this 'loss of face' that makes her look so ridiculous in the eyes of the world. By the same token, the one thing Etherege's characters seem unable to cope with is the expression of genuine emotion. When Dorimant is faced by Harriet, rather than, say, Loveit or some other mistress such as Belinda, he is completely at a loss. She rouses in him feelings of a different order of complexity from those he normally experiences in purely erotic encounters. But he is cautious of putting his feelings into words. To do so openly and, in so doing, to drop his protective mask, would be to risk exposure and possible humiliation. Harriet, for her part, is equally wary. She is well aware of how Dorimant, having enjoyed his mistresses, inevitably discards them. She is also aware, were she to marry him rather than become his mistress, that she would almost certainly be confined to her country estate in order to 'breed' and rear their family while Dorimant remained in London. Her dilemma, both emotionally and socially, is even more acute than his.

The play fittingly ends on an ambiguous note. Harriet states that she may be willing to engage herself more definitely if Dorimant shows enough commitment to visit her in the country: 'When I hear you talk thus in Hampshire, I shall begin to think there may be some little truth inlarg'd upon.' But there is no certainty that Dorimant will visit her in the country or that she will dare to drop her ironic mask even if he does. As far as Dorimant is concerned, it is far from clear whether he will ever find the confidence to approach Harriet as a real person rather than as a thing to be dominated and possessed. At the end of the play, neither Harriet nor Dorimant dare to trust their real feelings. Etherege's peculiar achievement was to depict their dilemma in all its poignance and complexity without inviting the audience to take up a judgemental position. Like Chekhov, he was painfully aware of the imperfections of his fellows, but he also saw and illustrated their thwarted potentiality.

The question-mark left at the end of *The Man of Mode* mirrored the question-mark that hung over Restoration England as a whole. It was a society torn by inner contradictions, an age in which Charles II and more blatantly after him, his brother, James II, attempted to impose on an increasingly middle-class, mercantile society the unwanted values of aristocratic absolutism. The experiment was doomed to failure. Rather like Chekhov's play, *The Cherry Orchard*, Etherege's *The Man of Mode* proved to be a pre-revolutionary work, faithfully recording the final spasms of a dying culture.

In contrast, Congreve's plays express the values of the new age following the Glorious Revolution of 1688 in which James II was ousted by William of Orange in a bloodless *coup d'état*. There was a quite different feel to the 1690s by comparison with the Restoration. During the course of that decade, English society seemed to find a new sense of purpose. It was not just the fact that a Bill of Rights guaranteed order and stability within the framework of a constitutional monarchy (a monarchy with clearly defined and circumscribed powers); there was also a new confidence and prosperity in the country, intimately linked with the growing power and authority of the merchant classes. The new merchant princes of London inhabited a world based upon the tangible realities of money and property: what mattered to them were contractual obligations, not inherited privileges. Their mode of operation was essentially pragmatic; their objective was the creation of personal wealth through the accumulation of capital investment. Congreve's work faithfully mirrors much of this, including the importance of money, property and contract.

In many ways, the Glorious Revolution of 1688 and its aftermath represented the triumph of middle-class beliefs and aspirations over those of aristocratic society. One manifestation of this was the growing influence of women and women's values within the community. Societies for the Reformation of Manners were founded during the 1690s and in these women played a leading role. Women also played a significant part in the campaign to purge the playhouses of the licence and bawdiness that had seemingly predominated on the stage since the Restoration. In the aftermath of Jeremy Collier's attack on the stage, a number of actors were prosecuted or threatened with prosecution

for uttering profane language on stage.[4] Collier himself chose to
continue his campaign against the stage by enlisting the support
of the fair sex in his open 'letter to a lady concerning the new
playhouse' (the Queen's Theatre in the Haymarket) in 1705.[5]

   Yet another sign of women's growing influence in society was
a significant change in the architectural lay-out of London's new
town houses. Prior to the 1690s, the interior disposition of town
and country houses mirrored the patriarchal values of society by
providing suites of rooms opening into each other, through which
the master of the house had unrestricted access. By the 1690s,
town and country houses in and around London were built around
a central grand staircase with separate rooms or suites of rooms
giving off the staircase and with corridors, rather than a series of
interconnected rooms, providing any additional points of entry.
This guaranteed the kind of privacy to the women of the house
that had been impossible previously. The social and psychological
significance of this change was deliberately highlighted by
Congreve in *The Way of the World* in 1700. At the end of her
list of provisos in the marriage contract scene of Act 4, Millamant
demands of Mirabell: 'And, lastly, wherever I am, you shall
always knock at the Door before you come in.' In earlier
Restoration comedies, such a demand would have been both
socially unlikely and architecturally impractical.

   Even divorce, which had hitherto been a taboo subject in polite
society and on the stage, began to figure as a serious topic of
concern by the turn of the century. Plays were written by both
Vanbrugh and Farquhar in the late 1690s and early 1700s
exploring the repercussions of disastrously unhappy marriages,
above all from a woman's perspective; and, in Farquhar's case,
addressing the actual issue of divorce. Vanbrugh's play *The
Provok'd Wife* offered a brilliant but ultimately cheerless
dissection of the anatomy of a marriage that has become
atrophied in a pattern of mutual vexation and unhappiness. Sir
John and Lady Brute have outlived any trace of mutual affection.
All that remains for them is to seek a series of escapes from each
other's company. In the case of Sir John, this means deliberate
neglect or verbal provocation of his wife, followed by a
continuous flight into an alcoholic stupor in the company of
drunken and loutish troublemakers; in the case of his wife, Lady
Brute, her escape route from verbal insult and injury leads her

towards the thought of an extramarital liaison. The play ends in an unresolved stalemate.

Farquhar's play *The Beaux' Stratagem* ostensibly records the attempt by two young gentlemen from London, Aimwell and Archer, to find wealthy brides in the country whose dowries will keep them in the style to which they have hitherto been accustomed. Aimwell duly finds his Dorinda, while Archer is attracted to Mrs Sullen who is already married, though most unhappily, to a country squire. Woven into this plot, in contrapuntal fashion, is the painfully accurate analysis of Mrs Sullen's unsuccessful marriage with Squire Sullen. Their life together is bleak in the extreme. He married to get heirs for his estate: she married for company and a shared social life. Neither has found what they want. Their marriage has remained childless and without the benefit of any genuine social intercourse. Squire Sullen prefers the company of regular drinkers in the alehouse to that of his wife and frequently comes home paralytically drunk in the early hours of the morning, only to disturb his wife's sleep and sweet dreams of better things. For her part, Mrs Sullen has no high expectations of marriage, but the drunken behaviour and taciturn neglect shown her by her husband drive her to distraction. As she comments to her sister-in-law Dorinda at the beginning of Act 2:

O Sister, Sister! If ever you marry, beware of a sullen, silent Sot, one that's always musing, but never thinks: – There's some Diversion in a talking Blockhead; and since a Woman must wear Chains, I wou'd have the Pleasure of hearing 'em rattle a little.

By the end of the play, their irreconcilable differences lead them to act out a ritual of divorce, or rather separation 'of bed and board', as full legal divorce was at the time effectively only available to the very wealthy in society.[6] *The Beaux' Stratagem* ends on a superficially happy note, but in reality none of the marital differences addressed in the play have been resolved. They have simply been papered over with a laugh and a dance and with more than a hint of sentimental character-drawing, particularly in the case of Aimwell and Dorinda who emerge as quite exemplary young lovers.

If Vanbrugh and Farquhar both reflect in their plays aspects of the new age, it is in Congreve's work that the ideals and values of post-revolutionary England are most clearly embodied. Without in any way subscribing to a sentimental view of human nature, Congreve manages to suggest in his late plays that human values can be preserved in an imperfect world and that there is a place for honesty and commitment despite human folly, greed and fickleness. It is above all his capacity for creating a tangible and credible sense of reality, a reality in which men and women can prosper, that sets him apart both from earlier Restoration writers and contemporary writers such as Vanbrugh and Farquhar. Even the Restoration figure of the licentious wild gallant becomes in Congreve's mature work a civilised and sophisticated man about town who is certainly capable of engaging in erotic adventures but whose ultimate aim is to find a relationship based upon mutual trust and commitment.

In his final play *The Way of the World* Congreve seems deliberately to make use of the settings, the themes and even the structural conventions of earlier Restoration comedies, only to rework and transform them into something both new and distinctively different.

The tavern or restaurant setting of earlier Restoration comedies, as, for instance, in *She wou'd if she cou'd,* which is regarded as a place for hard drinking and raunchy sex,[7] becomes a chocolate house in Act 1 of Congreve's play, an environment for social intercourse of an altogether more civilised nature. There is card play and conversation, banter and rivalry, but nothing resembling the Bacchic excesses of the earlier period.

Act 2 is set in St James's Park, reflecting the earlier period's fondness for contemporary London locations. But whereas for Etherege's characters, Hyde Park and the Mall were places for sexual assignations and adventures, for Congreve's characters, St James's Park is no more than a convenient place for a sociable walk before lunch, a gathering-point to meet friends, and a convenient place to pursue current concerns and plots.

The indoor settings of earlier Restoration comedies tend to be a series of different drawing-rooms in which a wide variety of people are received, underlining the essentially gregarious and outgoing nature of Restoration society. In contrast, the final three acts of Congreve's play take place in Lady Wishfort's house, underlining the sense of essentially family intrigue around which the whole play is structured.

As in earlier Restoration comedies, Congreve makes deliberate use of subplots that contrast effectively with the main action. For instance, the false wit (or limited vision) of characters such as Fainall, Marwood, Petulant and Witwoud, and the intrigues in which they are involved, is used to underline the true wit (or real insight) of the main characters Millamant and Mirabell, in much the same way that the minor characters in a Wycherley or Etherege play are used to enhance the stature of the main characters. Another device Congreve borrows, this time specifically from Etherege, is to delay the first entry of the heroine of his play, Millamant, until almost the end of Act 2. In *The Man of Mode*, Harriet's first appearance is not until Act 3. In both cases, imaginative responses to the character are stimulated in the audience's mind prior to her actual entry because she figures so frequently in the conversation of the other characters. The audience through this comes to share and understand something of the fascination exercised by the heroine in the mind of the hero well before she appears on stage.

The erotic games and sexual stereotypes to be found in earlier Restoration comedies are mirrored in Congreve's play. This leads him to show examples of duped husbands who are themselves deceivers; female machiavels who betray their best friends; older characters whose unstilled sexual appetite makes fools of them; and young couples warily assessing each other as possible partners. But there are also significant differences between his play and earlier Restoration comedies. Mirabell, for instance, is a wild gallant who has not simply discarded his former mistress, Mrs Fainall, but has given considerable thought to safeguarding her future. She, for her part, feels no bitterness towards her former lover, unlike some of the jilted heroines in earlier comedies, but uses her best offices to further his wooing of Millamant. Above all, against a background of fools and cheats, untrustworthy friends and potentially mercenary servants, Millamant and Mirabell stand out as a couple with a sophisticated grasp of the real world and its complexities. In both characters there is a potential for mature affection and commitment that goes well beyond the stage of an erotic game. Unlike the lustful leading characters of earlier Restoration comedies, Millamant and Mirabell are genuinely able to envisage the possibility of a lasting relationship based on mutual trust and respect for each other's freedom. But they are both hard-headed enough to realise that they will only achieve their goal with the help of rational strategies. Given the way of the world, mere affection is not enough: one also needs vigilance and forethought.

Congreve's play, in the elegant subtlety of its setting, structure and thematic content, mirrors the aristocratic tonality of Restoration writing, but its underlying temper belongs decisively to post-revolutionary England. *The Way of the World* represents the triumph of Whig moderation over aristocratic excess. In their different ways, Wycherley and Etherege reflected an old order, the final moments of a fading aristocratic culture. Congreve deliberately built into the fabric of his mature work the progressive values of the liberal merchant classes. His unique achievement was to do this with an unsentimental honesty that later writers were unable to match.

3
The Philosophical and Political Context

England throughout the seventeenth century experienced a profound sense of ideological clash and division, which led to civil war in the 1640s and revolution in the 1680s. Congreve wrote his plays in the final decade of what had been a turbulent century for English society. He himself was a dedicated supporter of the Whig cause and the ordered, constitutional vision of government it represented. As one might expect, his plays are firmly grounded in Whig values; they also reflect important aspects of the political debate that had raged throughout the century.

The debate centred on the issue of government: the nature, the function, the rights, the privileges and the obligations of government. Charles I's view of government involved him in a single-minded pursuit of a vision of divinely sanctioned kingship. This was in turn opposed by an equally strong-willed group of men passionately committed to the notion of constitutional, parliamentary rule. This clash led inexorably to the civil war that bitterly divided the nation in the 1640s. Even after the restoration of the monarchy in 1660, the debate rumbled on for the remainder of the century. Some of the major thinkers of the age took up firmly defined ideological positions in respect of the controversy and, in so doing, helped to focus the opinions and

views of their contemporaries, including contemporary playwrights. Congreve, for instance, was greatly influenced by the
thinking of the Whig philosopher, John Locke, who saw the
relationship between governed and government as essentially
contractual and therefore based on consent, not absolute authority. Such ideas are built into the fabric of Congreve's plays. But
there are also echoes, sometimes satirically coloured echoes, of
earlier Restoration thinking in his work. Indeed, it is impossible to
arrive at a proper understanding of his plays without viewing
them in the context of the ideas and events that had shaped
Restoration England.

After the Restoration of Charles II, the theatre and the
playwrights who wrote for it were understandably royalist and
therefore Tory by inclination. The work of dramatists such as
Etherege, Wycherley, Dryden, and Aphra Behn not only gives a
vivid picture of contemporary social behaviour and manners, but
inevitably reflects the ideas and values of royalist London in the
1660s and 1670s. This did not, however, lead to the writing of
simplistic propaganda plays. Playwrights of this stature were
committed to exploring some of the tensions and contradictions of
their society as well as celebrating its positive qualities. And even
within the royalist framework of thinking, there was division and
controversy, much of it centred on the writing of the philosopher,
Thomas Hobbes, who came to exercise a profound influence on
contemporary writers.

In his book *Leviathan* of 1651, published while he was in exile
in Paris, Thomas Hobbes had set out the first systematic analysis
of political theory. His aim was to establish the principles behind
good government so that the tragedy of civil war might never
again befall England. As a prelude to his political analysis,
Hobbes examined the wellsprings of individual human psychol-
ogy on the grounds that an understanding of human behaviour in
general would contribute significantly to an understanding of
human behaviour in a social and political context. His conclusions were startling. Looking at human behaviour from a
dispassionate, mathematical standpoint, Hobbes based his analysis of human conduct on the assumption that man was like any
other body in the physical universe and was therefore no more
than matter in motion. What this means in behavioural terms is
that man, as a sentient creature, responds to stimuli in such a way

as to gratify his appetite and avoid things that might cause him harm. Hobbes went on to assert that in his natural state man is a ruthlessly competitive creature, seeking to dominate his fellows in a ceaseless struggle for power:

> So that in the first place, I put for a generall inclination of all mankind, a perpetuall and restlesse desire of Power after power, that ceaseth onely in Death. And the cause of this, is not alwayes that a man hopes for a more intensive delight, than he has already attained to; or that he cannot be content with a moderate power: but because he cannot assure the power and means to live well, which he hath present, without the acquisition of more.[1]

Hobbes was well aware that his ideas were contrary to the accepted Christian notion of man as a being made in the image of God. He was equally aware that in the mechanistic universe he was sketching out there was no place for moral absolutes. Values of good and evil were entirely relative and entirely man-made:

> But whatsoever is the object of any mans Appetite or Desire; that is it, which he for his part calleth *Good*: And the object of his Hate, and Aversion, *Evill*; And of his Contempt, *Vile*, and *Inconsiderable*. For these words of Good, Evill, and Contemptible, are ever used with relation to the person that useth them: There being nothing simply and absolutely so; nor any common Rule of Good and Evill, to be taken from the nature of the objects themselves.[2]

Such a view of man as an amoral predator in a universe governed by the abstract laws of geometry might seem to leave little hope of achieving anything approximating to civil society. But for Hobbes, the reverse was true. As he saw it, to base political theory on anything other than a scientifically precise assessment of human behaviour at its potential worst, was to court disaster. Given his mechanistic view of human appetite and emotion, he argued that the only way of creating civil society was by persuading men freely to relinquish their natural inclination and right to achieve a position of dominance over others by vesting their individual power in a sovereign body or

individual whose authority should be absolute. The freely
accepted pre-eminence of such a sovereign entity was the only
guarantee of political stability and well-being. The alternative
was political anarchy and the kind of society where each and
everyone would have the right to challenge the authority of their
fellows by any available means. Understandably, Hobbes saw
recent events in England as a dire warning of the consequences of
such a state of war and he spelled them out in resonant terms:

> Whatsoever therefore is consequent to a time of Warre, where
> every man is Enemy to every man; the same is consequent to
> the time, wherein men live without other security, than what
> their own strength, and their own invention shall furnish them
> withall. In such condition, there is no place for Industry;
> because the fruit thereof is uncertain: and consequently no
> Culture of the Earth; no Navigation, nor use of the commodities
> that may be imported by Sea; no commodious Building; no
> Instruments of moving, and removing such things as require
> much force; no Knowledge of the face of the Earth; no account
> of Time; no Arts; no Letters; no Society; and which is worst of
> all, continuall feare, and danger of violent death; And the life of
> man, solitary, poore, nasty, brutish, and short.[3]

Hobbes's ideas had a considerable impact on his contemporaries. Understandably, they were vigorously opposed by the
Church. They were equally vigorously opposed by writers, such
as Dryden, whose strong Christian commitment led him to satirise
Hobbesian notions in a number of his heroic plays concerned with
political issues. Notably *The Conquest of Granada* seems full of
polemic argument against Hobbes's vision of man as matter and
hence appetite in motion.

Arguably the worst excesses of unbridled appetite are mani-
fested in the figure of the scheming female villain, Lyndaraxa,
who switches allegiance from one lover to the next, depending on
their changing status in the game of power politics. But even the
central figure of the two-part play, the conquering hero,
Almanzor, is represented as a man whose naive and uncontrolled
desires threaten the order and stability of civil society. It takes the
wise and witty Queen Almahide to teach him that 'all appetite

implies necessity', and is therefore a sign of weakness, whereas self-control and restraint are signs of strength and civilisation. Not surprisingly, Congreve, who had a warm admiration for Dryden the poet and an equally warm friendship with Dryden the man, shared the Poet Laureate's reservations in respect of Hobbes's ideas.

Hobbes's willingness in *Leviathan* to countenance *any* sovereign body, not just a monarch, did not endear him to traditional royalists with their belief in the divine right of kings. However, he enjoyed a favoured position at court, 'order was given that he should have free accesse to his majesty who was always delighted in his witt and smart repartees',[4] which ensured that his ideas were widely discussed and assimilated. Indeed, the plays of fashionable Restoration writers such as Etherege and Wycherley are populated with Hobbesian figures who struggle for power over each other: power measured by status, reputation, psychological and sexual domination and material possessions. Even laughter is construed in terms of power and dominance. In Etherege's *The Man of Mode*, for instance, Dorimant asks his friend Medley at an early stage in the play not to expose him to the ridicule of the town until he has had time to vindicate himself publicly.

Following the Glorious Revolution of 1688, Hobbes's ideas were displaced from their central position in the social and political thought of contemporary London. His arguments in favour of absolute authority, asserting its stabilising and beneficial effects for society as a whole, had a somewhat hollow ring in the light of recent political experience.

The rule of King James II had been an unmitigated disaster for the country. He was a king who had not flinched from using arbitrary powers in pursuit of his vision of divinely given authority. His commitment to Catholicism was as passionate as his view of kingship, and he was prepared to use any and every method, even extreme violence, to further both causes. Rebellions were bloodily suppressed; Anglican Privy Councillors and army officers were dismissed and replaced by Catholics; Parliament was prorogued for an indefinite term; and even the rule of statute law was formally suspended.[5] If this was what might be expected from a king committed to the notion of absolute and arbitrary authority, then it is hardly surprising that a number of leading political figures concluded that England would be better off without such a monarch. The final straw was the birth of a son to James in June 1688, which would ensure the continuation of Catholic rule.

It was at this point that William of Orange, who was married to the elder daughter of King James, was invited by a number of English noblemen to move against his father-in-law in order to protect the hereditary rights of his own wife, Mary. His 'invasion' of England, after landfall in Torbay on 5 November 1688, proved to be a popular move. Although his invading army was only half the size of the army under King James's command, the people rallied to his cause and James wisely decided to flee the country without joining battle. Even James's younger daughter, Anne, decided to join with his enemies.[6] After reaching London by mid-December, William was invited by a number of leading Whigs and Tories to call a Convention Parliament, which duly met on 22 January 1689. The upshot of this gathering was a resolution to the effect that King James had broken the original contract between the king and the people and had therefore abdicated. This left the way clear for the throne to be offered jointly to William and Mary, though with their powers limited by a Bill of Rights. In future, no monarch would be permitted to set aside the law of the land, nor to maintain a standing army during peace time; in addition, Parliament would have to meet regularly and could not simply be prorogued indefinitely.[7]

This settlement was widely welcomed. A number of high Tories opposed it, on the grounds that an anointed king could not lawfully be deposed; and a number of high-church clergymen accordingly refused to take the oath of allegiance to the new monarchs (in so doing earning themselves the title of non-jurors). In general, however, the Glorious Revolution of 1688 ushered in a period of stability and prosperity, both of which had been noticeably lacking during the supposedly divinely sanctioned but politically incompetent rule of James II.

All that now remained was to give the new regime the kind of philosophical respectability that had previously been enjoyed by the Stuart monarchs who had insisted so stubbornly on their God-given right to govern with absolute authority. The new political establishment needed an intellectually convincing apologia for what had been in effect a Whig-led rebellion against the principles and practice of absolute rule.

It was the philosopher, John Locke, who provided this much-needed vindication of the Glorious Revolution in his *Two Treatises of Government*, first published anonymously in 1690. Locke's avowed aim in the Preface was to found William III's claim to the throne on the consent of the people, and in so doing to build on Parliament's assertion that James II had broken the contract between the king and his subjects.

According to Locke, the whole notion of government depends upon the consent of the people, who enter into a voluntary contract with those who exercise authority, whereby they agree to abide by the majority decisions of government in return for the guaranteed preservation of their freedom and their property. Locke argued that man has a natural right to liberty and an equally natural right to property, and it is the duty of government to preserve these natural rights:

Man being born, as has been proved, with a Title to perfect Freedom, and an uncontrouled enjoyment of all the Rights and Priviledges of the Law of Nature, equally with any other Man, or Number of Men in the World, hath by Nature a Power, not only to preserve his Property, that is, his Life, Liberty and Estate, against the Injuries and Attempts of other Men; but to judge of, and punish the breaches of that Law in others, as he is perswaded the Offence deserves, even with Death it self, in Crimes where the heinousness of the Fact, in his Opinion, requires it. But because no *Political Society* can be, nor subsist without having in it self the Power to preserve the Property, and in order thereunto punish the Offences of all those of that Society; there, and there only is *Political Society*, where every one of the Members hath quitted this natural Power, resign'd it up into the hands of the Community in all cases that exclude him not from appealing for Protection to the Law established by it. And thus all private judgement of every particular Member being excluded, the Community comes to be Umpire, by settled standing Rules, indifferent, and the same to all Parties; and by Men having Authority from the Community, for the execution of those Rules, decides all the differences that may happen between any Members of that Society, concerning any matter

of right; and punishes those Offences, which any Member hath
committed against the Society, with such Penalties as the Law
has established . . . [8]

Government is thus an arbiter between men and is instituted for
the good of men and not for its own good. It has no absolute
power and has no justification for tyranny. It exists by contract
alone. Members of 'Political Society' agree to abide by majority
decisions of the community and its representatives in government
in order to ensure the preservation and safety of their freedom and
property.

Locke constantly stressed the importance of property, and in
this he foreshadowed the values of the new Whig mercantile class
of the eighteenth century. For him property was as important as
life and liberty. (Indeed his definition of property in the passage
quoted above suggests that for him property actually meant life
and liberty, as well as estate.) He was perfectly aware, given the
central importance of property to human society, that inequality
of possession of property would have to be justified if any kind of
stability, based on contractual values, was to be established. The
solution he found was both simple and elegant. Locke argued that
by using money (as opposed to relying on barter), men had tacitly
agreed to an unequal distribution of wealth, on the grounds that
money allowed a man to store and hence invest the products of his
land which he himself could not usefully consume. The argument
was pragmatic rather than equitable. But then Locke was less
concerned with establishing a system that was fair than with
creating a workable and reliable contractual base for the operation
of government. In this he succeeded with commendable adroit-
ness. Furthermore, his exposition of the importance of contract in
political society was to have a profound effect on many of his
contemporaries, including Congreve.

Congreve shared Locke's view that although the world was an
imperfect place, it could nevertheless be made habitable with the
help of binding contracts. *The Way of the World*, for instance,
presents us with an unvarnished image of society. We are shown
people who are often snide, vicious and deceitful, but through
contract they can be tamed and made sociable. Like Locke,
Congreve sees property and capital as the basis for all civilised
social intercourse; and it is contract that enables property to be

used. Without property and without contract, there would be no
social relationships and hence no civil society.
The *Way of the World* is full of contracts.
Fainall and his wife
are contracted on the basis of expediency on her part and financial
greed on his. Lady Wishfort desires to be contracted to Sir
Rowland in order to satisfy her itching if decayed sexual lust.
Waitwell is contracted to Foible in order to bind him closer to
Mirabell, while Sir Wilful pretends that he is willing to be
contracted to Millamant so as to help her in her affair with
Mirabell. All these contracts are false, based upon deception,
treachery or coercion. Only the contract between Mirabell and
Millamant is based upon consent, and it stands out all the more
because of this. Their relationship, which is predicated upon an
understanding of the perfidious way of the world, matures into a
tangible reality they both can trust because they both recognise
the validity and importance of contract. In the famous proviso
scene of Act 4, they itemise the detailed stipulations of a marriage
contract that will permit them to enter into obligations towards
each other, while still preserving a large measure of personal
freedom. Both characters, knowing each other's faults and the
faults of their world, are prepared to be contractually committed
to each other until death them do part.

The *Way of the World* is also very much concerned with
property. Both Mirabell and Millamant are aware that property is
essential, not for its own sake but as a means to physical well-
being. In order to have access to her property, kept from her by
her spiteful aunt Lady Wishfort, Millamant is prepared to deceive
friends and relatives. Such stratagems are unavoidable in an
imperfect world. Mirabell willingly engages himself and his
servants in the most elaborate schemes of deception in order to
help Millamant obtain control over her whole estate. In addition,
he has gone to great lengths to safeguard the property, and hence
the liberty, of his former mistress, Mrs Fainall. Her marriage of
convenience to Fainall (she badly needed a husband when she
feared that her affair with Mirabell had left her pregnant) could
have made her socially and financially vulnerable to a husband
whose every action was motivated by greed. On marriage, a
husband normally obtained absolute control over his wife's estate,
unless there was a marriage contract that specified the contrary.[9]
Mrs Fainall had sufficient confidence in Mirabell to make over to

him, in trust, the whole of her estate prior to her marriage to Fainall, which guaranteed her, if not happiness, at least a measure of independence and the possibility of exercising some control over her husband's greed and brutality. Here property is seen not simply as a means to physical well-being but as a restraining influence on potentially violent and destructive behaviour. Together, property and contract help to create the basis of civil society.

In *Love for Love*, Congreve had explored a similar range of ideas. There are false and true contracts; the greedy pursuit of property for its own sake is contrasted with the natural pursuit of property as a means to well-being; appetite is juxtaposed with self-control, sanity with madness. In addition, however, Congreve directs a deliberate attack on the Hobbesian views of a character from the previous generation, Sir Sampson Legend. Sir Sampson believes in absolute patriarchal authority and attempts to impose rigid control over his son, Valentine. As he expresses it in his own words:

> Why, I warrant my Son thought nothing belong'd to a Father, but Forgiveness and Affection; no Authority, no Correction, no Arbitrary Power; nothing to be done, but for him to offend, and me to pardon. [Act 2]

Needless to say, he fails. And he does so because his quick-witted son has a very clear grasp of the laws of contract. Valentine feigns madness at precisely the point in time when he has agreed, under duress, to sign away his right to inherit his father's estate in return for a much-needed cash payment to settle his current debts. (Even Hobbes had questioned the validity of agreements made under duress; for Locke, the absence of consent rendered an agreement null and void.)

Angelica, Valentine's beloved, shows an equally firm grasp of the law of contract. Faced by Valentine's madness (which is intended by Valentine as much as a test of her feelings towards him as it is a strategy to avoid signing Sir Sampson's conveyance), Angelica counterfeits an interest in Sir Sampson. Flattered and roused, Sir Sampson proposes a marriage contract that promises wealth and property in abundance, providing they have a child together. Angelica's reply sums up the hard-headed prudence of the new Whig generation: 'Let me consult my Lawyer concerning this Obligation; and if I find what you propose practicable, I'll give you my Answer' [Act 5]. Confronted by Angelica's seeming willingness to marry his own father, Valentine is prepared to admit that his madness was feigned and that he might now just as well sign his father's conveyance, given that his only interest in the estate was as a means to provide for a future life shared with Angelica. At this point, Angelica has received sufficient proof of Valentine's affection and can afford to declare her love for him and her willingness to bind herself contractually to him. At the same time, she openly criticises and mocks Sir Sampson for his wrong-headed belief that he had any kind of natural right to demand absolute obedience from his son:

Learn to be a good Father, or you'll never get a second Wife. I always lov'd your Son, and hated your unforgiving Nature. I was resolv'd to try him to the utmost; I have try'd you too, and know you both. You have not more Faults than he has Virtues; and 'tis hardly more Pleasure to me, that I can make him and my self happy, than that I can punish you. [Act 5]

In the freely given consent of Angelica and Valentine, the new age of contractually based relationships triumphs over the obsolete values of Stuart patriarchy. Sir Sampson, and his outmoded belief in divinely ordained authority, are firmly satirised in the closing scene of the play. To survive in this new period of hard-headed, mercantile values, one needs a lively wit to devise defensive strategies and a sound grasp of the importance of property and contract. Armed with these, Congreve and his Whig friends were convinced that men and women could prosper in an imperfect world and that despite 'the way of the world', there was a real place for honesty and commitment in personal and political relationships. Seen in this light, Congreve's plays represent, at the level of individual human interaction, a distillation of those values that had inspired people of all classes in the Glorious Revolution of 1688 to reject once and for all the notion that authority matters more than consent. If the rule of law depends on contract and consent, the same is true of all human relationships. Underneath the laughter and elegance of

Congreve's carefully contrived plays, one finds a shrewd political and social thinker at work who aligned himself firmly with the radical forces of his age.

4
The Theatrical Context

Congreve began writing during the reign of William and Mary. However his plays are normally labelled as belonging to the Restoration period in works of literary or theatre history. It is not difficult to see why. The theatres for which he wrote were initially those of Restoration England. In the 1690s, Wren's Theatre Royal, Drury Lane, was still the leading playhouse in London, while the Duke's Playhouse at Dorset Garden, though used less frequently, was nevertheless available for spectacular scenic productions. Equally the staging conventions of the Restoration theatre with its clear division between forestage and scenic stage were still utilised by contemporary playwrights: a forestage to which access was given by a pair of practical doors and on which most of the acting took place, and an upstage scenic area with wings and shutters providing a visual framework for the action.

In Restoration comedies, the painted shutters often depicted no more than stock interiors for much of the action, showing reception rooms or bedrooms in private lodgings and occasional tavern settings; the full scenic stage was opened up exclusively at one or two focal points in the play to show a contemporary outdoor location, often a park, such as Hyde Park, sometimes a street or arcade scene, such as Covent Garden or the New Exchange. Congreve used a variant of this pattern in his first comedy, *The Old Batchelour*, utilising a number of stock interiors and a neutral street scene for most of the action, and only exploiting the scenic stage, with a setting depicting St James's Park, briefly towards the end of Act 4. In *The Way of the World*, there is an even closer reference back to Restoration staging practice. Most of the action takes place in Lady Wishfort's lodgings. However, the play opens in a fashionable chocolate house (the nearest equivalent to the Restoration tavern); and Act 2 is set in St James's Park. Congreve skilfully exploits all the resources of the scenic stage to permit a number of interlocked scenes to pass swiftly in front of the spectator. The settings for his two other comedies written in the mid-1690s, *The Double Dealer* and *Love for Love* are confined to interior scenes, which may have been dictated by financial constraints and especially so in the case of *Love for Love*, which was first performed by an actors' company with severely limited financial resources.

In terms of setting, structure, and the use of theatre conventions, Congreve's plays are anchored squarely in the performance conventions of Restoration England. And yet his plays were written at a major turning-point in the development of the London theatre. What was changing was the composition of the audience and the type of repertoire needed to attract an audience. By the 1690s the court-based theatre of the Restoration, which had played to an educated and leisured élite, was giving way to a more discernibly commercial theatre, catering for a growing variety of tastes. Even the later starting-time for performances, between 5 and 6 p.m. after 1700 instead of 3.30 p.m. as at the Restoration, suggests that the theatre now expected to appeal to those who had spent the day working as well as those who were free to attend an afternoon performance. New forms of plays and entertainments were emerging to satisfy these tastes, including sentimental comedy, farcical afterpieces, and interludes of singing, dancing, acrobatics and pantomime. A flavour of this new kind of mixed repertoire is given in a travelogue published by a German visitor to London in 1710:

The comedy was played in Drury Lane. The theatre here is neither so large nor near as elegant as that in the Haymarket. Between every act they introduced several dances for variety, which is never done there. The above mentioned actress [Mrs Sandlow] danced charmingly as Harlequin, which suits her excellently and much pleases the English. They make such a to-do about her that her portrait in this costume is painted on snuff-boxes and frequently sold. After her a man appeared as Scaramouche, but he was far from being as elegant a dancer, though he excels in droll attitudes, leaping and contortions of the body, in which I never saw his equal [. . .] Finally a person with a horse, who was dressed as a mountebank or gypsy, came on to the stage and sang very well a long song, which was much clapped by the English.[1]

Although Congreve shared the political values of the new age, as a playwright his work belonged stylistically to the high comic traditions of Restoration England and was not designed to satisfy the middle-class preference for sentimental and intellectually less demanding material that was now beginning to make itself felt. Even at the outset of his playwriting career, it might be argued that Congreve was not entirely in sympathy with the direction that was being taken by the theatre of his time.

However, through his work as a playwright, he did become directly involved with the day-to-day activities of the contemporary theatre and its leading actors. In turn this led to his becoming embroiled in the major theatrical dispute of the period between the leading actors at Drury Lane and the manager of the theatre, Christopher Rich. The outcome saw Thomas Betterton and other leading actors from Drury Lane provoked into setting up a rival company and theatre in 1695 at Lincoln's Inn Fields.

The two theatre companies established in London at the Restoration had, since 1682, been amalgamated into one united company, which controlled both purpose-built theatres at Drury Lane and Dorset Garden. Despite the political instability of the 1680s, the company prospered under the firm guidance of its leading actor, Thomas Betterton. Difficulties began when the patent holder, Charles Davenant, sold his shares in the company in 1687 to his brother, Alexander. This event heralded a profound upheaval in the running of the company. Alexander introduced yet another brother, Thomas Davenant, as manager in place of Betterton and endeavoured to milk as much profit from the company as he could. Initially he had borrowed funds from an investor called Sir Thomas Skipwith in order to buy control of the company (although this was not made public at the time). Eventually he was obliged to sell off his shares to other investors including the lawyer, Christopher Rich, before finally fleeing from his creditors to the Canary Islands in 1693.

This period of instability had led to considerable unhappiness and even threats of mutiny amongst the actors of the united company. But that was nothing by comparison with the turmoil that ensued after Alexander Davenant's flight to the Canary Islands in 1693. It was at this juncture that the lawyer, Christopher Rich, and the investor or 'adventurer', Sir Thomas Skipwith, revealed the full extent of their financial interest in Drury Lane and took direct control of the company, as they were legally entitled to do so. Rich assumed responsibility for the day-to-day management and financial control of the company; his aim was to cut back all forms of expenditure, in particular the cost of salaries and wages, with a view to obtaining a guaranteed return on his personal investment. His strategy was to provoke some of the highly paid older actors, including Betterton and Mrs Barry into retirement, to strip away financial perks and privileges such as benefit performances or *ex-gratia* payments on retirement, and to ensure that his actors were paid on the basis of salary rather than as shareholders, which might have given them some say in the running of the company. The leading actors responded to these tactics by petitioning the Lord Chamberlain for redress in December 1694. Attempts at mediation were made but when it proved impossible to reconcile the parties to the dispute, and following an audience with King William III himself, the actors were granted a licence by the Lord Chamberlain to set up their own company and to move into their own theatre building. They accordingly opened their newly converted theatre in Lincoln's Inn Fields in April 1695 (the conversion being in part funded by a subscription raised from wealthy supporters).[2]

Congreve was firmly behind the actors in their dispute with Christopher Rich and the other patentees. His first two plays (*The Old Batchelour* and *The Double Dealer*) had been performed at Drury Lane, and by 1694 he was already negotiating with Rich over the production of his latest comedy, *Love for Love*. However, when the leading actors left Drury Lane to set up an actors' company, Congreve decided to offer them *Love for Love* for the opening of the playhouse in Lincoln's Inn Fields. Subsequently he agreed to become a shareholder in the new company, writing exclusively for them and offering them a new play every year 'if his Health permitted'.[3] In the event, he was to write only two plays (*The Mourning Bride* and *The Way of the World*) for the actors' company at Lincoln's Inn Fields before giving up his career as a playwright altogether.

This was only one of many disappointments that were to face the new actors' company. They started with high hopes and noble aspirations, organising themselves as a company of equal sharers in which no single individual was given overall managerial control. Their aim was to achieve a harmonious and supportive pattern of work through collective responsibility. The reverse seems to have happened: the lack of clear managerial control led to lax rehearsal discipline, sharp differences of opinion and other disorders. By 1700 the company was in such disarray that the Lord Chamberlain intervened and appointed Betterton to be in charge of the company although with limited disciplinary and financial powers.[4] Further problems were caused by the fierce competition from Rich at Drury Lane who was quite prepared to use his considerable financial resources to tempt audiences away from Lincoln's Inn Fields with lightweight farces, lavishly staged semi-operas and a variety of popular singers and dancers. By comparison, the actors at Lincoln's Inn Fields had limited financial resources which had to be husbanded very frugally. Even the initial sharers' agreement they had signed in 1695 made it clear that they had to meet their expenses entirely from their daily receipts:

The said parties being necessited to provide every thing anew for the Carrying on soe Great an undertakeing as all variety of Cloaths Forreigne habitts Scenes properties etc which must be paid out of the publique Receipts by the persons above named proportionable to the severall Shares & proportions each of them have in ye proffitts of the said playhouse.[5]

The main advantage enjoyed by the actors' company was their superior talent. Betterton, Mrs Barry and Mrs Bracegirdle were the undisputed stars of the age; the remaining sharers, namely Bowman, Underhill, Bright and Mrs Leigh were all experienced and accomplished performers. Although they too had to call on the services of popular singers and dancers to attract large audiences, they had the acting strength, in contrast to Drury Lane, to mount performances of demanding plays from the repertoire of Elizabethan and Restoration theatre.

Congreve benefited enormously from his association with these actors. He knew their strengths and weaknesses from his day-to-day contact with them, and in particular with Anne Bracegirdle. The parts he wrote were therefore tailor-made.

Betterton, the great tragic actor of the Restoration, was used by Congreve to give substance to some of his more scheming or cantankerous characters: Heartwell the surly old bachelor in the play of the same name; Maskwell, a villain in *The Double Dealer*, and Fainall, a treacherous and deceitful man about town in *The Way of the World*. It also seems likely that Sir Sampson Legend, the choleric father, in *Love for Love* was written with Betterton in mind, but in the chaos that ensued after the secession from Drury Lane, Betterton, now close to 60, was obliged to play the part of Sir Sampson's son, Valentine. In *The Mourning Bride*, Betterton played the role of the noble Osmyn.

Mrs Barry, the great tragic actress of the period, was used in a similar fashion. She too was given a series of difficult and demanding, though seemingly quite unflattering, roles in Congreve's comedies: Laetitia, whom Congreve described as a 'wanton and vicious character' in *The Old Batchelour*; Lady Touchwood, the unfaithful wife, in *The Double Dealer*; Mrs Frail, a promiscuous and unscrupulous woman about town in *Love for Love* and the deceitful Mrs Marwood, Fainall's mistress and pretended friend to Lady Wishfort, in *The Way of the World*. Even in *The Mourning Bride* Mrs Barry, given the role of Queen Zara, was asked to play the part of a woman whose passions were violently beyond control.

In contrast, Anne Bracegirdle was given the pleasing task of performing the roles of Congreve's various quick-witted and attractive heroines: Araminta in *The Old Batchelour*, Cynthia in *The Double Dealer*, Angelica in *Love for Love* and Millamant in *The Way of the World*. Contemporary descriptions make it clear that such roles were essentially vehicles for her to project her wit, her erotic charm and the mercurial complexity of her character. Colley Cibber, who was at the time a young actor at Drury Lane, commented in his memoirs:

When she acted *Millamant*, all the Faults, Follies and Affectations of that agreeable Tyrant, were venially melted down into so many Charms, and Attractions of a conscious Beauty.[6]

In Congreve's tragedy, *The Mourning Bride*, she was given another attractive role as the noble Almeria, Princess of Granada. On this occasion, however, one eighteenth-century writer, Anthony Aston, felt that she was overshadowed in her acting by Elizabeth Barry, 'Mrs Barry outshone Mrs Bracegirdle in the character of Zara in *The Mourning Bride*, although Mr Congreve designed Almeria for that favour.'[7]

Bowman played the role of the fop in three of Congreve's comedies: Lord Froth, a solemn coxcomb in *The Double Dealer*, Tattle in *Love for Love*, and Petulant in *The Way of the World*. Underhill excelled in male character parts such as Sir Sampson Legend in *Love for Love* or Sir Wilful Witwoud in *The Way of the World*; Elinor Leigh was equally successful in female character parts such as Prue's nurse in *Love for Love* and above all as Lady Wishfort in *The Way of the World*.

With these outstanding actors at his disposal, Congreve was able to promote and perfect an elegant and sophisticated form of satiric comedy, firmly rooted in the neoclassic traditions of Restoration playwriting. He could not have been better served by his actors. But neither he nor they were completely in tune with the way audience tastes were changing by the turn of the century. Their approach to acting, in perfect fusion with Congreve's style of writing, was informed by the love of wit, subtlety and discernment which had characterised the best of Restoration theatre. Unfortunately, the sensitivity and complexity informing their work were not uniformly appreciated by the kind of audiences attracted to London's theatres in the 1700s.

It was perhaps inevitable that Congreve's masterpiece, *The Way of the World*, should fail to please. In his dedication to Ralph, Earl of Montague, Congreve acknowledged that little of his play was designed to appeal to the current taste of audiences. Following the lukewarm reception given to his play, Congreve gave up playwriting altogether. Instead he turned his attention to other literary tasks, including the writing of masque and opera libretti. It may well have seemed to him that these genres at least were still guaranteed to appeal to an educated and informed audience who could appreciate allegorical and musical subtlety.

Once again it was for Anne Bracegirdle that he wrote the charming and pleasing role of Venus in his masque *The Judgement of Paris* (1701) which was set to music by four different composers in a splendid musical competition (described in Chapter 1). Anne was not only an accomplished actress, but a very fine singer. In fact the prompter Downes once declared that the effect of her singing was so magnetically charming that it, 'caus'd the Stones of the Streets to fly in the Men's Faces'.[8] Congreve was delighted with her performance.

This shift of focus in Congreve's work brought him close to Sir John Vanbrugh, a fellow-member of the Kit-Cat club, who was at the time planning to build London's first opera house. Vanbrugh was a well-known playwright as well as an architect. As a playwright, in comedies such as *The Relapse* and *The Provok'd Wife*, he excelled in astute character-drawing and the exquisitely precise dissection of unhappy marital relationships. In complete contrast, his work as an architect was marked by a delight in baroque extravagance. It was this quality that he brought to bear in designing his new play- and opera house, which was to be known as the Queen's Theatre in the Haymarket. He began work on the design in 1703 claiming in a letter to his friend Jacob Tonson that the interior was to be 'very different from any other house in being'.[9] He raised the building capital by a subscription of twenty-nine persons of quality who each paid a share of 100 guineas. Many of his friends in the Kit-Cat Club contributed.

At some stage in the planning process, Betterton agreed to move with his troupe of actors from Lincoln's Inn Fields to the new theatre on the understanding that he would then relinquish control of the company in favour of Vanbrugh. Betterton's role in the new company is far from certain. But by 1705 he was already 70 years of age and was keen to reduce his work load. There is some evidence that initially he continued to oversee new productions.[10] Congreve agreed to join with Vanbrugh as a patentee of the new theatre, although his projected role in the new company is even less clear. However, the two applied jointly to Queen Anne for a licence to operate the new playhouse. This was duly granted on 14 December 1704.

When the Queen's Theatre finally opened on 9 April 1705 with a production of an Italian pastoral opera, Jakob Greber's *The Loves of Ergasto*, the various disadvantages of Vanbrugh's ornate and flamboyant design were immediately apparent. Cibber described them as follows:

> Almost every proper Quality, and Convenience of a good Theatre had been sacrific'd, or neglected, to shew the Spectator a vast, triumphal Piece of Architecture! [. . .] For what could their vast Columns, their guilded Cornices, their immoderate high Roofs avail, when scarce one Word in ten, could be distinctly heard in it? [. . .] This extraordinary, and superfluous Space occasion'd such an Undulation, from the Voice of every Actor, that generally what they said sounded like the Gabbling of so many People, in the lofty Isles in a Cathedral - - - The Tone of a Trumpet, or the Swell of an Eunuch's holding Note, 'tis true, might be sweeten'd by it; but the articulate Sounds of a speaking Voice were drown'd, by the hollow Reverberations of one Word upon another.[11]

By December 1705, Congreve decided to cut his losses and sell his share in the theatre. This was the first of several departures or retirements by members of the original Lincoln's Inn Fields Company. George Bright followed in 1705, Anne Bracegirdle and John Verbruggen in 1707 (Betterton and Elizabeth Barry continued until 1710). Vanbrugh struggled on, in the face of vehement competition from Rich at Drury Lane. The next few years were turbulent and saw numerous complex changes in company structure and management. In 1707 Rich was given the exclusive right to mount musical productions in London as recompense for losing his best actors to Vanbrugh. A year later in 1708, Vanbrugh persuaded the Lord Chamberlain to reverse this decision and to give the Haymarket a monopoly of opera production in London. Apart from the fact that his theatre was better suited acoustically to operas than to plays, he presumably made this move on the assumption that audiences would be prepared to pay inflated prices to come and hear the internationally famous singing stars he was proposing to engage; but not enough people were willing to pay the kind of prices he needed to charge in order to balance his books. In the spring of 1708

Vanbrugh was no longer able to pay all his creditors, and relinquished control of the theatre to his manager, Owen Swiney; in the process he had accumulated substantial debts that were to burden him for many years to come.[12]

Vanbrugh's disappointment was hardly more bitter than Congreve's. Vanbrugh had designed a flawed playhouse, whereas Congreve in *Semele* had written an opera libretto for its opening that was a worthy rival to the approach taken in Italian opera. Once again, he had conceived the leading role for Anne Bracegirdle and in so doing may well have intended to demonstrate her pre-eminence as a potential opera singer. (Her probable disappointment at the eventual failure to have the opera produced at Drury Lane in the winter of 1707 may have contributed in some measure to her decision to retire prematurely from the stage at that point in time.) Through the sequence of events outlined in Chapter 1, Congreve was denied the satisfaction of seeing his opera in production. He must have been galled by the thought that, without a production of *Semele*, London's theatres were offered no convincing alternative to the Italian operas that were now beginning to flood in. His libretto, with its intelligent and thoughtful reworking of a classical myth, was in every way superior to the arid formality of the Italian operas now offered to London audiences. Congreve exploited a variety of poetic devices, including verbal wit and visual suggestion as well as deliberately lush imagery, to explore themes of erotic love, ambition and jealousy in a full-blooded and passionate manner. Through Eccles's tardiness in composing the music and because of Vanbrugh's difficulties with his flawed playhouse, London audiences were denied the opportunity to compare the merits of a specifically English style of opera with that of the Italians.

Handel's arrival in London in 1711 confirmed the triumph of the Italian mode. He was to supply the music for a long list of Italian opera settings throughout his lengthy career as a London-based composer. (It is interesting to note, however, that not even Handel and the luminaries of the Royal Academy of Music, established in 1719 with the help of generous royal and aristocratic subvention, could make the production of Italian opera in London a viable commercial undertaking.) It was also Handel who was to provide something of a vindication of Congreve's approach to the writing of opera libretti. In 1744 he

took Congreve's libretto of *Semele* as the basis for one of his
Lenten oratorios. A contemporary librettist helped to tone down
some of Congreve's more suggestive passages. Although the
work failed to please contemporary puritan sensibilities, particularly in a Lenten context, Handel's magnificent musical setting
brought out all the power and complexity of Congreve's text and
indicates what Congreve might have achieved in collaboration
with a major composer. (The operatic qualities of Handel's
'oratorio' were amply demonstrated in the 250th anniversary
production of *Semele* mounted by the Royal Opera House in
1982.)[13]

If it was Handel who provided the vindication of Congreve's
approach as an opera librettist, it was Goldsmith and Sheridan
writing in the 1770s who furnished the vindication of his
approach as a playwright. After decades in which the genre of
sentimental comedy had predominated on the London and
provincial stages, they successfully revived the satiric tradition
in comedy to which Congreve had been so committed. In plays
such as *She Stoops to Conquer* and *The Rivals* one finds echoes
of individual Congreve characters. Kate Hardcastle in *She Stoops
to Conquer* is a hard-headed young lady reminiscent of Angelica
in *Love for Love* and is, like her, determined to put her would-be
suitor to a severe test before finally accepting him. Lydia
Languish in *The Rivals* is an admittedly far more superficial
but equally mercurial version of Millamant in *The Way of the
World*. Her lover, Captain Jack Absolute, is as bemused by her
behaviour as is Mirabell in response to Millamant. Jack's father,
Sir Anthony Absolute, is very reminiscent of Sir Sampson Legend
in *Love for Love*. There is also in Goldsmith and Sheridan a
similar commitment as in Congreve to a probingly honest
exploration of human interaction in a contemporary social
context.

Although Congreve may have failed to win his artistic battles in
the theatre of his own age, his example clearly provided a fertile
source of inspiration for later playwrights and composers.[14] He
wrote at a turning-point in theatre history. In many ways, the
subtlety of his work, the themes and conventions he used, as well
as the actors for whom he wrote, all belonged to a previous age.
And yet the artistic quality and integrity of his playwriting was
such that it continued to fascinate actors and audiences through-

out the major part of the eighteenth century. Three years after Congreve's death, John Rich chose to open his new Theatre Royal in Covent Garden on 7 December 1732 with a production of *The Way of the World*, in which, 'pit and boxes were laid together at 5*s* – first gallery at 2*s* – upper gallery at 1*s* – and to prevent the scenes from being crowded, admission on the stage was raised to half a guinea'.[15]

Clearly, the play's subtlety and its complexity of texture were no longer daunting to London audiences. John Rich's symbolic gesture in opening his new playhouse in 1732 with *The Way of the World* (echoing Betterton's choice of another Congreve comedy, *Love for Love*, to open the new theatre in Lincoln's Inn Fields in 1695) confirmed Congreve's reputation as the finest writer of satiric comedy of wit and helped to establish a firm place for his plays in the repertoire of the Georgian theatre.

5
Literary Theory and Morality Debates

In his dedication to *The Way of the World*, Congreve outlined his admiration for the work of the Roman dramatist Terence. By implication he also associated himself with a playwright whose approach to writing was akin to his own. In Congreve's view, what distinguished Terence's writing was its precision and correctness. Significantly he also felt that 'the Purity of his Stile, the Delicacy of his Turns, and the Justness of his Characters, were all of them Beauties, which the greater Part of his Audience were incapable of Tasting'. [vol 3, p. 10] This was exactly the predicament in which Congreve found himself in 1700. His whole approach to playwriting was based on an intimate acquaintance and profound sympathy with the classical tradition and its values of subtlety, decorum and precision. These values were woven into the fabric of his own work, but it seemed to him that the contemporary world, as in Terence's case, was incapable of appreciating them.

Not only had his latest comedy *The Way of the World* met with a lukewarm response from London audiences in 1700, but in addition, for the previous two years, Congreve had been subjected to a sustained and aggressive critical assault. In 1698 his plays, along with those of other contemporary writers including Dryden, Durfey and Vanbrugh, had been exposed to ridicule and censure in the work of a non-juring priest, Jeremy Collier, entitled *A Short View of the Immorality and Profaneness of the English Stage*. Further pamphlets and attacks had followed this initial offensive, including Collier's own *Defence of the Short View*. Some of the attacks were coarse and abusive. Under these circumstances, it is hardly surprising that Congreve felt his contemporaries were incapable of appreciating the subtlety in his work on which he prided himself.

Outraged at the fatuous quality of the attack on him, Congreve had been provoked into publishing, somewhat unwisely, a vigorous rebuttal of Collier's critique in his *Amendments of Mr Collier's False and Imperfect Citations* (1698). In the process, he found himself dragged down to Collier's level in much of his essay, notably in his lengthy analysis of Collier's inflated view of the importance of the clergy. However, the opening sections are used to good effect to set down in summary his perception of the form and function of comic writing, and as such provide the best starting-point for an exploration of Congreve's conception of comedy.

He begins by establishing four fundamental reference points (or *postulata*, as he calls them) for a sound critical understanding of comedy. In the first of these, he sets out the Aristotelian base for his view of comedy:

> Comedy (says Aristotle) is an Imitation of the worse sort of People. [. . .] He does not mean the worse sort of People in respect to their Quality, but in respect to their Manners. [. . .] there are Crimes too daring and too horrid for Comedy. But the Vices most frequent, and which are the common Practice of the looser sort of Livers, are the subject Matter of Comedy. He tells us farther, that they must be exposed after a ridiculous manner: For Men are to be laugh'd out of their Vices in Comedy; the Business of Comedy is to delight, as well as to instruct: And as vicious People are made asham'd of their Follies or Faults, by seeing them expos'd in a ridiculous manner, so are good People at once both warn'd and diverted at their Expence. [vol. 3, p. 173]

A number of important points emerge from this paragraph. Above all, it serves to underline the fact that Congreve, as a

writer of comedies, sees himself working firmly within the
neoclassic satiric tradition derived from Aristotle. As part of
that tradition, Congreve affirms that the function of comedy is to
offer delight as well as instruction. Its object is to satirise follies
and faults by subjecting foolish or vicious behaviour to ridicule.
Within such a framework there is no scope for introducing the
kind of exemplary characters demanded by Collier and his
followers.

In the second of his postulates, Congreve explains that his
characters have a life of their own. It is his task as a comic writer
to show characters behaving and talking foolishly or viciously.
But it must not be assumed that his own views coincide with those
of such characters. The point at issue here is that an author's
intentions are rarely expressed in the words given to an individual
character, but rather that they emerge contextually.

In his third postulate, Congreve elaborates on the importance of
a contextual understanding of comic dialogue. What matters is
not simply what is said, but rather which character says a given
line, to whom, and for what purpose:

> I must desire the impartial Reader, not to consider any
> Expression or Passage cited from any Play, as it appears in
> Mr *Collier's* Book; nor to pass any Sentence or Censure upon it,
> out of its proper Scene, or alienated from the Character by which
> it is spoken; for in that place alone, and in his Mouth alone, can
> it have its proper and true Signification. [vol. 3, p. 173]

In stressing the importance of a contextual reading of a given
scene, Congreve once again was basing his approach on sound
Aristotelian precept. In Chapter 25 of *The Poetics* Aristotle had
established that the dramatic context of an action or statement
was the only means of determining whether an action or statement
was morally good or bad.

In the fourth of his postulates, Congreve returns yet again to the
question of dramatic context, this time in respect of the alleged
profanity in his plays:

> Because Mr *Collier* in his Chapter of the Profaneness of the
> Stage, has founded great part of his Accusation upon the
> Liberty which Poets take of using some Words in their Plays,

which have been sometimes employed by the Translators of the Holy Scriptures: I desire that the following Distinction may be admitted, *viz.* That when Words are apply'd to sacred things, and with a purpose to treat of sacred things; they ought to be understood acordingly: But when they are otherwise apply'd, the Diversity of the Subject gives a Diversity of Signification. [vol. 3, p. 174]

The charge of profanity levelled against Congreve could only be sustained if it were clear from the context in which a given speech or phrase occurs that the author intended to mock the divine. The reverse is true. When one of Congreve's characters makes light of phrases with a religious resonance, what is satirised is not the divine, but the behaviour of the character or the responses of other characters, and it is the context that establishes this fact. Furthermore, as Congreve points out, words used in different contexts have different meanings. It is part of the stock-in-trade of the comic dramatist to exploit the subtle nuances of meaning that can be derived from this insight.

The notion of comedy that is conveyed in these four postulates is complex and multifaceted. Repeatedly Congreve stresses the importance of context. Words only acquire their true significance when they are seen and understood in their proper context; characters can only be understood in the context of their interaction with others; an author's intentions can only be inferred from the context of the work in its entirety and not from an isolated phrase. In comedy, meaning and significance are relative, not absolute, values: they emerge from the whole process of interaction between author, actor and audience. Without the creative participation of an audience using their wit and perception to understand character, dialogue and action contextually rather than at a literal-minded and face-value level, there is no laughter and hence no comedy.

Prior to the writing of his *Amendments*, Congreve's views on comedy had been scattered throughout his work, notably in a letter written in 1695 to the critic, John Dennis, *Concerning Humour in Comedy*, and in various dedications to his plays. What emerges from these disparate observations is a craftsman's fascination with the basic building blocks of comic writing.

In his essay, *Concerning Humour in Comedy*, Congreve shows a clear understanding of the importance of the humours tradition in English comic writing and offers a definition of what is meant by the term 'humour' that is obviously inspired by both Ben Jonson and John Dryden:

I take it to be, *A singular and unavoidable manner of doing, or saying any thing, Peculiar and Natural to one Man only; by which his Speech and Actions are distinguished from those of other Men.* [vol. 3, p. 165]

In the same essay, he takes great pains to distinguish humour both from wit and from affectation. As he explains, wit is often mistaken for humour (as is its opposite, folly). But wit is something quite different. It is a manner of response that may be used by a character rather than a determining feature affecting the whole behaviour of the character. As Congreve expresses it:

a Character of a Splenetick and Peevish *Humour* should have a Satyrical wit. A Jolly and Sanguine *Humour* should have a Facetious Wit. The Former should speak Positively; the Latter, Carelessly: for the former Observes, and shews things as they are; the latter rather overlooks Nature, and speaks things as he would have them; and his *Wit* and *Humour* have both of them a less Alloy of Judgment than the others. [vol. 3, p. 162]

Affectation is likewise often mistaken for humour. But affectation is an acquired or learned folly rather than a natural or instinctive pattern of behaviour. Congreve acknowledges that good comic writing, 'may be drawn from Affectations', but the most demanding kind of comic writing involves, in his view, the subtle exploitation and juxtaposition of contrasting humours:

Nor is it only requisite to distinguish what Humour will be diverting, but also how much of it, what part of it to shew in Light, and what to cast in Shades; how to set it off by preparatory Scenes, and by opposing other Humours to it in the same Scene. [vol. 3, pp. 166–7]

This amounts to something close to a blueprint for his own comic writing and indicates the seriousness with which he viewed his task as a playwright, which was to make a 'Comedy true in all its parts, and to give every Character in it a True and Distinct Humour'. [vol 3, p. 167]

Other aspects of comic writing are dealt with in the dedications to his plays. In his dedication to *The Double Dealer*, for instance (which was written as a somewhat prickly response to the robust criticism the play had encountered), Congreve stressed the importance he attached to neoclassic principles of structural purity and simplicity:

> I confess I design'd (whatever Vanity or Ambition occasion'd that design) to have written a true and regular Comedy [. . .] And now to make amends for the vanity of such a design, I do confess both the attempt, and the imperfect performance. Yet I must take the boldness to say, I have not miscarried in the whole; for the Mechanical part of it is perfect. That, I may say with as little vanity as a Builder may say he has built a House according to the Model laid down before him; or a Gardiner that he has set his Flowers in a knot of such or such a Figure. I design'd the Moral first, and to that Moral I invented the Fable, and do not know that I have borrow'd one hint of it any where. I made the Plot as strong as I could because it was single, and I made it single because I would avoid confusion, and was resolved to preserve the three Unities of Drama, which I have visibly done to the utmost severity. [vol. 2, pp. 9–10]

The sense of working within a clearly defined neoclassic tradition is unmistakable here. Without any trace of false modesty, Congreve claims to have followed a neoclassic blueprint – what he calls 'the Mechanical part' of playwriting – with perfect precision. The play is structured in such a way as to conform to the letter to the neoclassic demand for unity of action, time and place. The ability to write with such regularity is, in Congreve's view, part of the essential craft of playwriting.

He goes on to defend his use of satire, and in particular his satiric treatment of some of the female characters in the play:

some of the Ladies are offended [. . .]. They are concerned that I have represented some Women vicious and affected. How can I help it? It is the business of a Comick poet to paint the Vices and Follies of Humane kind; and there are but two sexes that I know, *viz*. *Men* and *Women*, which have a Title to Humanity: And If I leave one half of them out, the Work will be imperfect. I should be very glad of an opportunity to make my Complement to those Ladies who are offended; but they can no more expect it in a Comedy than to be Tickled by a Surgeon when he's letting 'em blood. They who are Virtuous or Discreet should not be offended, for such Characters as these distinguish them, and make their Beauties more shining and observ'd: And they who are of the other kind, may nevertheless pass for such, by seeming not to be displeased or touched with the Satyr of this *Comedy*. [vol. 2, pp. 11–12]

Underneath the elegant gibe at those members of the fair sex who felt threatened by the way he had depicted certain female characters in the play, Congreve relies once again on a neoclassic definition of the satiric function of comedy to defend his approach.

There is an unmistakable tone of impatience in this and other dedications as Congreve writes in vindication of his neoclassic view of playwriting in response to a contemporary world from which he felt increasingly alienated. The sense of isolation is most acute in the dedication to his final play, *The Way of the World*, in which he sees himself at odds with contemporary taste and its preference for simplistic and coarse comic effects:

Those Characters which are meant to be ridiculous in most of our Comedies, are of Fools so gross, that in my humble Opinion, they shou'd rather disturb than divert the well-natur'd and reflecting Part of an Audience; they are rather Objects of Charity than Contempt; and instead of moving our Mirth, they ought very often to excite our Compassion. [vol. 3, p. 9]

In contrast, what Congreve sees himself as offering in his comedy is a work of subtlety and complexity in which he has taken as the object of his satire a number of characters who embody in their behaviour 'an affected Wit; a Wit, which at the same time that it is affected, is also false' [vol. 3, p. 9]. Congreve admits that such an approach to character-drawing is fraught with difficulty and is also liable to misunderstanding, which is exactly what happened.

In general, the ideas expressed in these various dedications supplement and reinforce the quintessentially neoclassic view of comedy outlined in his *Amendments*. By the time he wrote the dedication to *The Way of the World*, Congreve was fully aware that the tide of public opinion had turned. His contemporaries, it seemed, no longer properly appreciated the satiric vision of comedy that informed his work and instead preferred a style of comedy that was based on a moralising and sentimental approach. It was hardly surprising that the tone of his dedication was distinctly valedictory.

The shift in public sensibility that may be discerned in the late 1690s was in part a reflection of the puritan tastes of William III and his court and in part an indication of the growing importance of London's mercantile classes whose puritan commitment had changed little throughout the seventeenth century. The renewal of assertive puritan thinking during the 1690s made people receptive to the ideas of Jeremy Collier. In many ways, however, Collier was an unlikely champion of middle-class puritan ideology.

Collier was a dedicated Jacobite whose spirited defence of James II implied that William III was an illegal usurper of the English throne. Having spent some time in prison because of such political views, Collier finally succeeded in getting himself branded as an outlaw by attending two men on the scaffold (and offering them absolution) who were condemned to death because of their involvement in a plot to assassinate the King. Collier was an extremist, a professional renegade, who thrived on controversy. His whole life seems to revolve around endless pamphlet wars. By the late 1690s, however, he had boxed himself into a corner; any further political writings might have cost him his life. He wisely decided instead to turn his attention to contemporary playwrights. He brought to the world of criticism the same delight in combative polemics that he had displayed in his political pamphlets. He nevertheless managed to sum up ideas in his work that were very much in the air at the time.

The basic critical concepts informing his *Short View* were derived from various prescriptive French critics of the seventeenth century, notably Rapin. In their turn, they were to be echoed in the work of English and continental critics throughout the eighteenth century, in particular Lessing and Diderot. From the outset, Collier made it clear that he saw playwriting as having primarily a didactic function:

> The business of *Plays* is to recommend Virtue, and discountenance Vice; To Show the Uncertainty of Humane Greatness, the suddain Turns of Fate, and the Unhappy Conclusions of Violence and Injustice: 'Tis to expose the Singularities of Pride and Fancy, to make Folly and Falsehood contemptible, and to bring everything that is Ill under Infamy and Neglect.[1]

Collier vehemently rejected the notion that delight ought to be the main object of comic writing. As he saw it, this opened up the way to each and every kind of abuse, with even the most valuable and honourable things in life liable to be exposed to laughter. Instead, what he wanted was a clear-cut critique of vicious and anti-social behaviour leading to a poetically just distribution of punishments and rewards by the end of a given play:

> The exposing of Knavery, and making *Lewdness* ridiculous, is a much better occasion for Laughter. And this with submission I take to be the End of *Comedy*. And therefore it does not differ from *Tragedy* in the *End*, but in the *Means*. Instruction is the principal Design of both. The one works by Terror, the other by Infamy.[2]

Clearly, within such a definition of comedy, there is no room for subtlety and poetic ambiguity. Repeatedly, Collier demonstrates in his detailed critiques of scenes from a variety of plays, including those by Congreve, that he has no conception of subtextual or contextual meaning:

> In the *Old Batchelour*, *Vain-love* asks *Belmour*, *Could you be content to go to Heaven?*
> *Bell. Hum, Not immediately in my Conscience, not heartily –*
> This is playing I take it with Edge-Tools. To go to Heaven in

jest, is the way to go to Hell in earnest. In the Fourth *Act*,
Lewdness is represented with that Gaity, as if the Crime was
purely imaginary, and lay only in ignorance and preciseness.
*Have you throughly consider'd (says Fondlewife) how
detestable, how heinous, and how crying a Sin the Sin of
Adultery is? Have you weighed [it] I say? For it is a very
weighty Sin: and altho it may lie [heavy upon thee] – yet thy
Husband must also bear his part; For thy Iniquity will fall on
his Head.* I suppose this fit of Buffoonry and Profaneness, was
to settle the Conscience of young Beginners, and to make the
Terrors of Religion insignificant. *Belmour* desires *Laetitia to
give him leave to swear by her Eyes and her Lips*: He Kisses
the Strumpet, and tells her, *Eternity was in that Moment.*
Laetitia is horribly Profane in her Apology to her Husband; but
having the *Stage-Protection* of Smut for her Guard, we must
let her alone. *Fondlewife* stalks under the same shelter, and
abuses a plain Text of Scripture to an impudent Meaning. A
little before, *Laetitia* when her Intrigue with Belmour was
almost discover'd, supports her self with this Consideration. *All
my comfort lies in his Impudence, and Heaven be prais'd he
has a Considerable Portion.* This is the *Play-House* Grace, and
thus Lewdness is made a part of Devotion.[3]

Characters and dialogue are viewed in isolation; quotations are
taken out of context; foolish or vicious characters are seen as
mouthpieces for their author's views; all behaviour is interpreted
at a literal-minded level. In addition, Collier engages in a
painstaking witch hunt for any trace of profane or licentious
language. Indeed such is his zeal that it is difficult to avoid
concluding that he had something of a prurient fascination with
profanity and immorality. (Some of his opponents reached the
same conclusion, as for instance, the anonymous author of *A
Vindication of the Stage* who asserted, 'His Dwelling so long on
the Subject of Debauchery, argues something of Delight and
Pleasure in the case'.)[4]

Collier's real motives in writing the work were almost certainly
political. In the first place, he needed to find some degree of
rehabilitation in society, having been outlawed for his opposition
to William III. This aim was achieved in full: the Protestant

monarch, William III, was so impressed by Collier's *Short View* that he issued a *nolle prosequi* in respect of Collier's political misdemeanours.[5] Second, in attacking Congreve, Collier was able to denounce a writer whose firm commitment to Whig ideology and the Glorious Revolution that had deposed James II made him an obvious target for Jacobite venom. This point was not lost on Congreve's friends. The anonymous author of *Some Remarks upon Mr Collier's Defence* wrote:

> All my Acquaintance that discourse this Matter, are convinced Mr *Collier* has a particular Pique against Mr *Congreve*; nay, some will go farther, and guess the Cause; perhaps there may be Lines of that Author's that vex the *Non-Juror* more than all the smutty Jests he has pickt up; Lines that Mourn the Royal *Pastora*; Heroick Lines, that sound the Glory of our Monarch.[6] From this sweet Poetry they judge his Gall is raised; which being gorged and full, overflows, nor spares the dead or living, Friends and Foes, the bitter Deluge reaches and bespatters all.[7]

Despite these mixed motives, Collier's work was very popular with middle-class readers who felt little or no affection for the stage and who heartily disliked those writers of satiric comedy who had for years mocked their puritan values and life styles. Thus it was that Collier the Jacobite, the unrepentant Stuart royalist, became the champion of puritan middle-class sensibility: an extraordinary alliance that was to have a decisive influence on the initial development of theatre criticism in England as it emerged as a distinctive critical genre in the first two decades of the eighteenth century.

Collier's popularity paved the way for men such as Addison and Steele who were, in contrast to him, staunch Whigs but who wanted to see the theatre reformed in line with middle-class puritan sensibilities. Together they launched a journal called *The Tatler* in April 1709 for which Steele wrote a number of essays on theatrical subjects. The tone of these essays (the first examples of published theatre criticism in England) is generally relaxed and conversational; at one point, Steele even distances himself from the committed reformers in his review of *The Country Wife* performed at Drury Lane in April 1709:

I cannot be of the same Opinion with my Friends and Fellow-Labourers, the *Reformers of Manners*, in their Severity towards Plays, but must allow, that a good Play, acted before a well-bred Audience, must raise very proper Incitements to good Behaviour, and be the most quick and most prevailing Method of giving Young People a Turn of Sense and Breeding.[8]

However, by the time Steele came to write for *The Spectator* in 1711, he had clearly been won over by the reformist camp. The sententious zeal he displays is at times almost indistinguishable from that of Collier. His most vituperative piece is a critique of Etherege's comedy *The Man of Mode*:

I will take for granted, that a fine Gentleman should be honest in his Actions, and refined in his Language. Instead of this, our Hero, in this Piece, is a direct Knave in his Designs, and a Clown in his Language. *Bellair* is his Admirer and Friend, in return for which, because he is forsooth a greater Wit than his said Friend, he thinks it reasonable to perswade him to Marry a young Lady, whose Virtue, he thinks, will last no longer than 'till she is a Wife, and then she cannot but fall to his Share, as he is an irresistible fine Gentleman. The Falsehood to Mrs *Loveit*, and the Barbarity of Triumphing over her Anguish for losing him, is another Instance of his Honesty, as well as his good Nature. As to his fine Language; he calls the Orange Woman, who, it seems, is inclined to grow Fat, *An Over-grown Jade, with a Flasket of Guts before her*; and salutes her with a pretty Phrase of, *How now, Double Tripe?* Upon the Mention of a Country Gentlewoman, whom he knows nothing of (no one can imagine why), he *will lay his Life she is some awkward, ill-fashioned Country Toad, who not having above four Dozen of Hairs on her Head, has adorned her Baldness with a large white Fruz, that she may look Sparkishly in the Fore-front of the King's Box at an old Play.* Unnatural Mixture of senseless Common Place! [. . .] To speak plainly of this whole Work, I think nothing but being lost to a Sense of Innocence and Virtue can make any one see this Comedy, without observing more frequent Occasion to move Sorrow and Indignation, than Mirth and Laughter. At the same time I allow it to be Nature, but it is Nature in its utmost Corruption and Degeneracy.[9]

The influence of Collier is unmistakable: the critical methodology and vocabulary are the same. The critic chooses a play he dislikes, measures it against an *a priori* puritan moral code and finds it wanting; scenes, characters and lines of dialogue are then paraded out of context to prove the author's depravity of view and purpose. Finally, the play in question is consigned to outer darkness because it is regarded as being beyond the pale of polite society. Like Collier, Steele had no understanding or appreciation of satiric comedy and its aims. In his view, satiric comedy, by showing negative examples of behaviour, was merely an invitation to wickedness and vice. As a critic and a playwright, what he wanted to see was a reformist style of comedy with exemplary characters and scenes of sentimental poignance that would reinforce the overall positive message of a play.

His fellow-playwright and actor, Colley Cibber, had shown the potential for such an approach to playwriting in his comedies, *Love's Last Shift* (1696) and *The Careless Husband* (1704). Indeed in his dedication to the latter play, Cibber made it clear that he was deliberately attempting to meet a contemporary desire for reformist plays:

> The best Criticks have long and justly complain'd, that the coarseness of most characters in our late Comedies, have been unfit entertainments for People of Quality, especially the Ladies: and therefore I was long in hopes that some able pen (whose expectations did not hang upon the profits of success) wou'd generously attempt to reform the Town into a better taste than the World generally allows 'em: but nothing of that kind having lately appear'd, that would give me an opportunity of being wise at another's expence, I found it impossible any longer to resist the secret temptation of my vanity, and so even struck the first blow myself: and the event has now convinc'd me, that whoever sticks closely to Nature, can't easily write above the understanding of the Galleries, tho' at the same time he may possibly deserve applause of the Boxes.[10]

Where Cibber was content to respond to contemporary taste in his playwriting, Steele wished to pursue a more deliberately reformist policy in his essays and his plays. He wrote a number of moderately successful reformist comedies in the early 1700s, *The Funeral* (1701), *The Lying Lover* (1703) and *The Tender Husband* (1705), and then returned to the stage in the early 1720s with his play, *The Conscious Lovers* (1722), in which he set the pattern for the improving and sentimental comedies of the eighteenth-century stage. In his preface to this play, dedicated to no less a person than King George I, Steele outlined the aesthetic justification for his sentimental approach to playwriting:

> The chief Design of this was to be an innocent Performance, and the Audience have abundantly show'd how ready they are to support what is visibly intended that way; nor do I make any Difficulty to acknowledge, that the whole was writ for the sake of the Scene of the Fourth Act, wherein Mr *Bevill* evades the Quarrel with his Friend; and hope it may have some Effect upon the *Goths* and *Vandals* that frequent the Theatres, or a more polite Audience may supply their Absence.
> But this Incident, and the Case of the Father and Daughter, are esteem'd by some People no Subjects of Comedy; but I cannot be of their Mind: for any thing that has its Foundation in Happiness and Success, must be allow'd to be the Object of Comedy; and sure it must be an Improvement of it, to introduce a Joy too exquisite for Laughter, that can have no Spring but in Delight, which is the Case of this young Lady. I must therefore contend, that the Tears which were shed on that Occasion flow'd from Reason and good Sense, and that Men ought not to be laugh'd at for weeping, till we are come to a more clear Notion of what is to be imputed to the Hardness of the Head, and the Softness of the Heart.[11]

The notion of exemplary characters whose behaviour may help to exert a positive influence on 'the Goths and Vandals that frequent the Theatres', allied to the championing of 'a Joy too exquisite for Laughter' in comic writing, could not be further removed from Congreve's pursuit of stylistic purity and satiric honesty. The gulf between these two approaches is immense and indicates just how far eighteenth-century sensibilities had shifted since Congreve had written his plays and had set down his ideas on comic theory.

However, the victory enjoyed by the reformers was far from clear-cut. Satiric comedies, including Congreve's, retained their popularity on the eighteenth-century stage; robust farces and afterpieces were often far more popular than new-style sentimental comedies; even the critical debate between supporters and opponents of a sentimental approach continued to reverberate throughout the century.[12] The aesthetic values in which Congreve believed may have been derided by some of his more vociferous contemporary opponents, but their validity was acknowledged by discerning theatre managers, actors, audiences and critics throughout the Georgian era.

6
Comedies of Appetite and Contract

A number of themes and issues recur throughout Congreve's work: arguably the most persistent is his concern with the destructive power of appetite. In his later plays Congreve explores how reason and contractually based order can together counteract or at least restrain the deleterious effects of appetite and impulse. In the unstable world governed by appetite, chaos and disorder is an ever-present threat; but his heroes and heroines in his later plays find a way of establishing order and stability in their relationships partly through having a clear conception of their objectives and partly through using prudent strategies to achieve these objectives.

THE OLD BATCHELOUR

In complete contrast, Congreve in his first play, *The Old Batchelour*, engaged in a high-spirited exploration of the world of appetite, viewed from an essentially festive and youthful perspective. This is a play that reads almost like a straight throw-back to the world of early Restoration comedy. At its centre one finds Bellmour, a wild gallant in pursuit of Belinda, an affected young society lady. The vigour of the chase does not, however, prevent Bellmour from engaging in a number of other sexual escapades worthy of Etherege's Dorimant. His friend, Vainlove, serves as the perfect foil to Bellmour. Vainlove enjoys the chase but not the consummation. Twice he has handed on his conquests for his friend to clinch the act of consummation; and in both cases (the women concerned are Silvia and Laetitia) his friend Bellmour has had to use disguise to press home his advantage. Vainlove meanwhile is engaged in a relationship with a thoughtful young lady called Araminta who wisely keeps him at arm's length.

Although the main focus of the play is on these two young couples and their mutual sparring, a number of other plots are woven around their intrigues. There is Heartwell, the surly old bachelor, who gives the play its title; he is in danger of making a complete ass of himself by marrying Silvia, a less than virginal young lady. She has previously offered herself to Vainlove, only to find Bellmour taking up her generous offer under cover of darkness. Bellmour in his turn saves Heartwell from this disastrous marriage by himself conducting the marriage service dressed up as a puritan preacher. Having thus prevented her marriage with his friend Heartwell, Bellmour finds a suitably wealthy but foolish husband for Silvia in the shape of Sir Joseph Wittol. Sir Joseph and his friend, Captain Bluffe, are another pair of characters who drop in and out of the action as and when it suits the dramatist. They are a pair of perfectly matched fools: Sir Joseph, a witless and foppish country knight who has more money than either sense or discretion, and Bluffe, a boasting coward who hides his cowardice behind the time-honoured mask of a braggart soldier. These two are beaten and cheated at regular intervals in the action and are finally gulled into marriage with respectively the far from virtuous Silvia and her no less sexually experienced maid, Lucy.

Apart from a pimping servant called Setter and an opportunist friend called Sharper, there are two other characters who briefly cross Bellmour's path: Fondlewife, a rich but impotent old banker, and Laetitia, his sexually frustrated young wife. As in the case of Silvia, Laetitia has made an assignation with Vainlove, only to find Bellmour (disguised as a puritan preacher) appearing in Vainlove's place. Such is her frustration that she takes little persuasion to accept him as a suitable substitute. As ill luck would have it, Fondlewife returns home just as they have completed their coupling, and it takes all of Bellmour's verbal wit and dexterity to convince Fondlewife, against his better judgement, that he is not a cuckold when quite plainly he is.

At the end of the play, the Fondlewifes are forgotten; Sir Joseph and Bluffe are resigned to their respective marriages; Heartwell is relieved that he has escaped from a disastrous match and that he remains an unmarried bachelor; Araminta wisely still resists Vainlove's less than wholehearted amorous pleas; while Bellmour plunges rashly into marriage with Belinda, still flushed as he is from his latest sexual escapades with the lustful Laetitia.

Even from this compressed outline of the plot, it will be clear that there is very little obvious unity of action in the play. Events seem to follow a loose kaleidoscopic pattern, mirroring the life style of the main character Bellmour who tumbles blithely from one experience to the next. There is, however, a general dramaturgic logic underpinning the action, which seems derived from the example of Jonson as mediated and commended by Dryden in his essay *Of Dramatic Poesy*.[1] In his analysis of Jonson's play *The Silent Woman*, Dryden commented appreciatively on the way Jonson had knit together the action of his play and had enlivened the action with a pleasing variety of characters and subplots:

> But that the poet might entertain you with more variety all this while, he reserves some new characters to show you, which he opens not till the second and third act [. . .] all which he moves afterwards in by-walks, or under-plots, as diversions to the main design, lest it should grow tedious, though they are still naturally joined with it, and somewhere or other sub-servient to it.[2]

This is very much the pattern Congreve has followed in his writing of *The Old Batchelour*. Although the action may at a superficial first glance appear to be a fortuitous jumble of events, it is in fact modelled on the practice and principles of England's foremost neoclassic playwright.

The remaining two neoclassic unities of time and place are given due regard in the play. The action is completed within the course of a single evening; indeed the play reads as the light-hearted escapades of a summer's night. Much of the action also takes place 'in the Street', a clear reference back to Serlio's street-scene settings for Italy's first neoclassic plays of the sixteenth century. Congreve has little difficulty in compressing the action into the confines of a summer's night, but occasionally the street is vacated in favour of either Silvia's or Laetitia's chamber.

Generally, the mood of the play is light-hearted. There is none of the brooding violence or cruelty of Jonson's world, despite the structural borrowings from Jonson's work. The destructive potential of appetite is shown, but Congreve does not dwell on the dangers. The play feels like the work of a young writer who is content to show us other young people coasting through experiences without stopping for long to consider the consequences of their actions.

There are some dark moments of near-disaster, as, for instance, when Heartwell, the surly bachelor of the title, is almost trapped in a ruinous marriage with the wayward Silvia. Even before he walks in through her front door, he knows he is making a grave error of judgement. In an amusing but revealing soliloquy, he has to command his rebellious feet to move:

Well, why do you not move? Feet do your Office – Not one Inch; no, Foregod I'me caught – There stands my North, and thither my Needle points – Now could I curse my self, yet cannot repent. O thou Delicious, Damn'd, Dear, destructive Woman! 'Sdeath, how the young Fellows will hoot me! I shall be the Jest of the Town: Nay, in two Days, I expect to be chronicled in Ditty, and sung in woful Ballad, to the Tune of the *Superanuated Maidens Comfort*; or, *the Batchelor's Fall*; and upon the third, I shall be hang'd in Effigie, pasted up for exemplary Ornament of necessary Houses and Coblers Stalls – Death, I can't think on't – I'le run into the danger to loose the apprehension.

[Act 3, vol. 1, p. 188]

He is saved from his impetuous folly by pure coincidence: Bellmour happens to be walking along the road, disguised as a puritan cleric, at precisely the same moment as Lucy is sent out by Silvia to find a priest who can marry her to Heartwell.

A little later in the action, before Heartwell discovers that his supposed marriage service was in fact a sham, he is subjected to savage mockery by his young friends, and in particular by the young ladies. He is so incensed that he actually threatens to draw his sword against Belinda:

> HEARTWELL: Death, Am I made your Laughing-stock? For you, Sir, I shall find a time; But take off your Wasp here, or the Clown may grow boistrous, I have a Fly-flap.
> BELINDA: You have occasion for 't, your Wife has been blown upon.
> BELLMOUR: That's home.
> HEARTWELL: Not Fiends or Furies could have added to my vexation, or any thing, but another Woman – You've wrack'd my patience; begone, or By –
> BELLMOUR: Hold, hold. What the Devil, thou wilt not draw upon a Woman?
>
> [Act 5, vol. 1, p. 221]

The moment of panic soon passes and Heartwell forgives his young friends their mirth when he learns that they have in fact been protecting his interests all along by saving him from the misery of a disastrous marriage.

Another dark moment occurs in the play when the banker, Fondlewife, returns home to find Laetitia, his wife, with a supposed cleric in her chambers. He is inclined to believe her tale that Mr Spintext, the puritan preacher, has been taken with a sudden fit of the colic and is lying down on her bed to recover. But then he discovers the supposed Mr Spintext's reading matter: not a prayer-book but Scarron's novelette, *The Innocent Adultery*. As Bellmour comments ruefully:

> Damn'd Chance! If I had gone a-Whoring with the *Practice of Piety* in my Pocket, I had never been discover'd.
>
> [Act 4, vol. 1, p. 209]

Bellmour responds to the situation by making a brazen confession in which truth and lies are inextricably woven together:

In short then, I was informed of the opportunity of your absence, by my Spy (for Faith, honest *Isaac*, I have a long time designed thee this favour) I knew *Spin-text* was to come by your direction – But I laid a trap for him, and procured his Habit; in which, I pass'd upon your Servants, and was conducted hither. I pretended a Fit of the Cholick, to excuse my lying down upon your Bed, hoping that when she heard of it, her good Nature would bring her to administer Remedies for my Distemper. – You know what might have follow'd. – But like an uncivil Person, you knock'd at the Door, before your Wife was come to me.

[Act 4, vol. 1, p. 211]

Fondlewife is fully aware that Bellmour's tale is false. But the alternative to believing it, as Bellmour reminds him, is a public scandal and the ensuing separation of himself from his wife. He chooses the less painful option. This time disaster is averted not by pure chance but by enlightened self-interest. Fondlewife prefers to retain the *status quo* rather than face the humiliation of scandal and separation. Bellmour comments laconically:

See the great Blessing of an easy Faith; Opinion cannot err.

No Husband, by his Wife, can be deceiv'd;
She still is Vertuous, if she's so believ'd.

[Act 4, vol. 1, p. 212]

Meanwhile, he himself is still determined to press on with marrying his Belinda who is unlikely to prove more faithful to him than he to her.

Such dark moments are few and far between. For the most part, the play offers an attractive blend of fast-moving action and sparkling dialogue. Indeed much of the effect of the play depends upon verbal wit, and it was this that made it an immediate success when it was first performed. The dialogue is self-consciously clever; it is full of similes and fanciful images, as the various characters score off each other in witty repartee. There are true wits of both sexes who are past masters at verbal fencing; and there are dull wits whose use of language is always amusingly inappropriate to the specific situation in which they find themselves. The true wits know how to manipulate language to their own ends; they also know how to hide their real feelings behind the words they use. This is especially true of the two young couples at the centre of the play who are past masters at verbal sniping; Araminta, in particular, knows how to wield a verbal rapier with exquisite dexterity. In the following extract, she even knows when to call a halt to a bout of verbal fencing that threatens to get out of hand:

BELLMOUR: [. . .] I have laid out such a world of Love in your Service, that you think you can never be able to pay me all: So shun me for the same reason that you would a Dun.

BELINDA: Ay, on my Conscience, and the most impertinent and troublesome of Duns – A Dun for Mony will be quiet, when he sees his Debtor has not wherewithal – But a Dun for Love is an eternal Torment that never rests –

BELLMOUR: Till he has created Love where there was none, and then gets it for his pains. For importunity in Love, like importunity at Court; first creates its own Interest, and then pursues it for the Favour.

ARAMINTA: Favours that are got by Impudence and Importunity, are like Discoveries from the Rack, when the afflicted Person, for his ease, sometimes confesses Secrets his Heart knows nothing of.

VAINLOVE: I should rather think Favours, so gain'd, to be due Rewards to indefatigable Devotion – For as Love is a Deity, he must be serv'd by Prayer.

BELINDA: O Gad, would you would all pray to Love then, and let us alone.

VAINLOVE: You are the Temples of Love, and 'tis through you, our Devotion must be convey'd.

ARAMINTA: Rather poor silly Idols of your own making, which, upon the least displeasure you forsake, and set up new – Every Man, now changes his Mistress and his Religion, as his Humour varies, or his Interest.

VAINLOVE: O Madam –

ARAMINTA: Nay, come, I find we are growing serious, and then we are in great danger of being dull – If my Musick-master

be not gone, I'll entertain you with a new Song, which comes
pretty near my own Opinion of Love and your Sex.
[Act 2, vol. 1, pp. 184–5]

The fanciful images used by one character are taken up by the
next and turned against the original speaker; one barbed comment
trumps another until the moment when Araminta is finally
provoked into speaking the truth, which is the one thing that is
not acceptable. Viewed from the perspective of wit, to speak the
truth is to be both serious and dull, and is therefore to be avoided
at all costs. True wit requires men and women paradoxically to be
economical with the truth, particularly when feelings and
emotions are involved. If, for instance, Bellmour and Belinda
were to speak the truth to each other, there would be no
possibility of any relationship between them. They are therefore
cautious of revealing too much of their real feelings either to each
other or to their friends. Both of them in public profess to view
marriage as a penance, or at best, as Belinda puts it, as 'a very dull
play'; and yet they deliberately plunge into a marriage with each
other. The only hope for them both is that somewhere, in the
unspoken gap between truth and wit, there is room for genuine
affection and commitment. This may seem something of a slender
hope but at least Belinda is inclined to dream of her lover,
Bellmour, and call out his name in her sleep (as Araminta reminds
her), and Bellmour has a very real interest in Belinda's substantial
personal fortune, as he frankly confesses to Sharper at the
beginning of the play. On Belinda's part there is then some
evidence of a romantic attachment to Bellmour (even he has
noticed this); while, for his part, he has a very deep respect for her
property. Taken together, these two responses may just add up to
a viable marriage of some kind, but the omens are far from
convincing.

Each of the characters has his or her own distinctive brand of
wit. Belinda's is extravagant; Araminta's restrained and polished;
Bellmour's erratic and Vainlove's ironic. Heartwell, on the other
hand, tends to use mocking comparisons. Even the gulls and
dupes are allowed their own particular brand of false wit. Bluffe
invariably hides behind military imagery; Sir Joseph has a
fascinating stock of mild expletives, 'Gads–Daggers–Belts–

Blades–and–Scabbards, this is the very Gentleman!'; while
Fondlewife has a sophist's ability to tie himself in knots with
tortured prose and equally tortured arguments:

> Tell me *Isaac*, why art thee Jealous? Why art thee distrustful of
> the Wife of thy Bosom? – Because she is Young and Vigorous,
> and I am Old and Impotent – Then why didst thee Marry *Isaac*?
> – Because she was beautiful and tempting, and because I was
> obstinate and doating; so that my inclination was (and is still)
> greater than my power – And will not that which tempted thee,
> also tempt others, who will tempt her *Isaac*? – I fear it much –
> But does not thy Wife love thee, nay, doat upon thee? – Yes –
> Why then! – Ay, but to say truth, She's fonder of me, than she
> has reason to be; and in the way of Trade, we still suspect the
> smoothest Dealers of the deepest designs – And that she has
> some designs deeper than thou canst reach, th' hast experi-
> mented *Isaac*.
>
> > [Act 4, vol. 1, p. 198]

Throughout the play, the dialogue crackles and fizzes, while the
gulls are duped: Heartwell is saved from his own folly, Fondlewife cuckolded, Silvia sexually deceived and then palmed off on
Sir Joseph, Araminta resists Vainlove, and Belinda rushes into
marriage with Bellmour. There is also ample theatrical action of a
robust, almost farcical nature. Beatings and whoring are both
physically portrayed. Sharper, for instance, gives Bluffe a beating
in the style of Punch and Judy, which he is too cowardly to return
or even protest about. While Bellmour's frank admission that he
loves the whole female sex is no idle boast. Even as he pays
verbal court to Belinda, he engages in intimate physical contact
with Laetitia who offers no more than token resistance to his
sexual advances. The whole play is full of sheer, raw energy,
including sexual energy, which provides actors and actresses with
ample opportunity physically to fill out and flesh out their
characters.

Viewed as an artistic whole, *The Old Batchelour* is a play that
has none of the exquisite balance of Congreve's later work. There
is no rational restraint to counterbalance the effects of unbridled
appetite; there is no sense of real or even potential stability
underpinning the responses of the young couples in the play.

(Even Belinda makes this point in her dissection of Bellmour's courtship in Act 5 [vol. 1, p. 219]: 'You are so curious in the Preparation, that is, your Courtship, one wou'd think you meant a noble Entertainment:- But when we come to feed, 'tis all Froth, and poor, but in show.') What the play offers instead of any discernibly mature or solid values is youthful exuberance and a light-hearted exploration of a mode of behaviour that Congreve later came to view as essentially dangerous and destructive. It was a zestful but uncharacteristic start to his playwriting career; and it was one that pleased the town enormously.

THE DOUBLE DEALER

In *The Old Batchelour* Congreve offered a light-hearted and festive exploration of the world of appetite. In his next play *The Double Dealer*, the festive mood is fractured by a conspiracy in which passion and villainy act together in a distinctly unholy alliance. In this play the consequences of giving in to unbridled appetite are spelled out with brutal clarity. Appetite can destroy both family and social stability; it is a cancer that gnaws at the very fabric of all relationships and can have disastrous repercussions.

In *The Double Dealer* relationships are no longer seen as a series of youthful games to be played out on the street, but rather as the essential building blocks of family and social life. And yet families, like society at large, are fragile things. Congreve shows them made up of weak-willed, vain human beings who deceive themselves and who are in turn deceived. For the most part, family relationships leave much to be desired, but there is a conservative force that keeps families and marriages together despite their imperfections. Only when unrestrained appetite takes over is the conservative fabric of family and marital life really threatened. These are the concerns at the very heart of Congreve's play.

As the author himself points out in his dedication, the play follows a strict neoclassic pattern, complying with the unities of time, place and action.[3] The whole action takes place in and around the gallery in Lord Touchwood's house; there is a hint in the dialogue that it may be a country residence near St Albans. It is compressed into a few hours and is primarily concerned with the attempt by two individuals, Lady Touchwood and Maskwell, to prevent Mellefont, the young hero of the play, from marrying Cynthia to whom he is betrothed. The framework for the action is a house-party given by Lord Touchwood to celebrate his nomination of Mellefont, his nephew, as his sole heir on the eve of Mellefont's marriage to Cynthia Plyant. Cynthia's father, Sir Paul Plyant, is already related to Lord Touchwood through marriage as Lady Touchwood is Sir Paul's sister. This forthcoming marriage between Mellefont and Cynthia will accordingly bind together two powerful families, both with considerable property and wealth, even more strongly than before. Its importance is further underlined by the fact that neither Lord Touchwood nor Sir Paul has a son. (Both Lord Touchwood's and Sir Paul's marriages are in every sense barren.) The marriage of Mellefont and Cynthia therefore offers both families a genuine hope of stable and ordered inheritance for the future.

Mellefont and Cynthia are no ordinary young lovers: they already carry on their shoulders the burden of considerable financial and dynastic responsibility. Hardly surprisingly, they do not engage in the light-hearted banter of the young couples from Congreve's previous play. They are far more mature and thoughtful in their responses to each other. Understandably, the responsibilities of marriage loom large in their minds. In the few scenes they have together, Cynthia in particular worries about the commitment she is about to make to Mellefont. The following exchange from the middle of Act 2 is typical:

> CYNTHIA: 'Tis an odd Game we're going to Play at: What think you of drawing Stakes, and giving over in time?
>
> MELLEFONT: No, hang't, that's not endeavouring to Win, because it's possible we may lose; since we have Shuffled and Cutt, let's e'en turn up Trump now.
>
> CYNTHIA: Then I find it's like Cards, if either of us have a good Hand it is an Accident of Fortune.
>
> MELLEFONT: No, Marriage is rather like a Game at Bowls: Fortune indeed makes the match, and the Two nearest, and sometimes the Two farthest, are together, but the Game depends entirely upon Judgment.

CYNTHIA: Still it is a Game, and Consequently one of us must be a Loser.

MELLEFONT: Not at all; only a Friendly Tryal of Skill, and the Winnings to be shared between us.

[Act 2, vol. 2, p. 30]

Cynthia is astute enough to realise that all relationships follow a changing pattern of winning and losing. The prospect of becoming a permanent loser is one that worries her. Mellefont sees things differently. For him, the challenges of marriage are like a friendly match in which winning or losing is less important than the game itself, and both players will share together any winnings. The image is a benevolent one and is indicative of his generous temperament. They are indeed a well-matched and fundamentally wholesome young couple who are treated in an almost idealised manner by the author. This makes them closer to the flawless young couples of sentimental comedy than it does to the carefree couples of the Restoration. This impression is strengthened by the way Mellefont's friend, Careless, responds to them: his behaviour is a model of solidarity and support, anticipating the warm and generous friendships of later sentimental comedies.

The world these characters inhabit is populated with fools and dupes, most of them harmless and ineffectual representatives of a ruling class who are totally preoccupied with their own narrow and essentially trivial concerns. Lord and Lady Froth epitomise the way in which triviality can be elevated into an almost balletic art form:

LADY FROTH: My Lord, I have been telling my dear *Cynthia* how much I have been in Love with you; I swear I have; I'm not ashamed to own it now; ah! it makes my heart leap, I vow I sigh when I think on't. My dear Lord! Ha, ha, ha, do you remember, my Lord?
[*Squeezes him by the hand, looks kindly on him, sighs and then laughs out.*]

LORD FROTH: Pleasant Creature! Perfectly well, ah! that look, ay, there it is; who could resist? 'twas so my heart was made a Captive first, and ever since t' has been in Love with happy Slavery.

LADY FROTH: Oh, that Tongue, that dear deceitful Tongue! that Charming Softness in your Mien and your Expression, and then your Bow! Good my Lord, bow as you did when I gave you my Picture; here, suppose this my Picture. [*Gives him a Pocket-Glass.*] Pray mind, my Lord; ah! he bows Charmingly; nay, my Lord, you sha'n't kiss it so much; I shall grow jealous, I vow now.

[*He bows profoundly low, then kisses the Glass.*]

LORD FROTH: I saw my self there, and kis'd it for your sake.

LADY FROTH: Ah! Gallantry to the last degree.

[Act 2, vol. 2, pp. 28–9]

Despite their fulsome protestations of love, Lady Froth is easily seduced by the vapid Brisk who is nevertheless astute enough to flatter her by admiring her painfully limited poetic skills. Having flirted and danced with her, he ends up teaching her about the stars as she lies on her back and gazes up at them over his shoulder.

Cynthia's father, Sir Paul Plyant, is hardly any better. Cynthia is his daughter from his first marriage. His second marriage is a travesty. Lady Plyant refuses to sleep with him except when she fears she may be pregnant from one of her extramarital affairs. To her husband she offers an image of nice chastity; she insists that he sleep with his body and arms tightly wrapped up in a swathe of blankets so that he cannot come near her. But faced by lusty young lovers she is easily persuaded. She is even prepared to contemplate sleeping with her future son-in-law, when Maskwell and Lady Touchwood spread the false rumour that Mellefont fancies her more than Cynthia. Meanwhile, Sir Paul accepts the few crumbs of comfort she throws him and puts up with her snubs and snide comments; he even permits her to give him a spending allowance from his own estate. Mellefont is greatly bemused, as he describes his future father-in-law to his friend Careless in Act 3:

swaddled up in Blankets, and his hands and feet swath'd down, and so put to bed; and there he lies with a great beard, like a *Russian* bear upon a drift of Snow. [Vol. 2, p. 42]

So much for the fools. The villains of the piece are Lady Touchwood and Maskwell. Lady Touchwood is a passionate adulteress who throws aside all the accepted laws of civil and familial obligation to pursue her sexual obsession for her nephew, Mellefont. She has thrust her unwanted attentions on him on numerous occasions; the most recent being that very morning when she burst into his bedroom and ended up threatening him with a sword. On other occasions her fury at being slighted by him has led her to plot against him and seek to diminish him, by every conceivable means, in his uncle's eyes. Meanwhile she has consoled herself sexually with Maskwell who is in service with her husband (presumably as a private secretary or steward). Together they use the rhetoric of passion, but what they practise is pure lust.

Maskwell is a devious and scheming underdog, a seeming friend to Mellefont who has used his good offices to obtain for Maskwell a place in his uncle's establishment. But Maskwell is the falsest of friends who is eaten up by jealousy and vanity and whose only passion is to prove himself superior to those he serves and to those who regard him as a friend. Maskwell is so obsessed with his own cunning that he regards nothing as sacred and will sacrifice anything and anybody to his appetite for power and status. With Lady Touchwood he plots Mellefont's downfall, but he also plots to his own advantage how best to arrange that he, and not Mellefont, shall marry Cynthia, without Lady Touchwood discovering his intentions. The technique that Maskwell uses is to tell his victims the truth without them realising that he is engaged in an act of double bluff:

> Why, *qui vult decipi decipiatur.* – 'Tis no fault of mine: I have told 'em in plain terms how easie 'tis for me to cheat 'em, and if they will not hear the Serpent's hiss, they must be stung into experience and future caution. [Act 5, vol. 2, p. 69]

Mellefont is no match for the world of passion and villainy opposing him. Although he knows that his aunt will use every strategy against him, and is therefore alert and on guard, he foolishly trusts Maskwell who is the main agent of his destruction. His one real friend, Careless, has an instinctive dislike of Maskwell and suspects his involvement with Lady Touchwood: Mellefont brushes these objections aside and is subsequently manipulated by Maskwell like so much putty. Finally he faces disgrace and banishment to outer darkness. Lady Touchwood has claimed to her husband that Mellefont has incestuous designs upon her. Maskwell engineers a piece of brilliant theatre in Lady Touchwood's bedroom that will give Lord Touchwood the proof he wants. Mellefont lies concealed there. Lady Touchwood begins her sexual foreplay with Maskwell, which is Mellefont's cue to burst in on them. Maskwell, however, slips away through a secret passage which permits him to fetch Lord Touchwood. Even as Mellefont has Lady Touchwood seemingly in his power, having disturbed her *in flagrante* with Maskwell, she catches sight of her husband and instantly begins accusing Mellefont of making incestuous advances. Totally defeated, Mellefont finds himself confronted by the horrendous prospect of having Maskwell replace him as Lord Touchwood's heir and Cynthia's future husband.

Even now, Mellefont still trusts Maskwell. The more Maskwell reveals his real designs to him, the more Mellefont trusts him. Increasingly he seems too gullible and credulous to be a true man of wit. No wonder Cynthia at one point in the action demands that he prove his wit to her. Mellefont appears completely at sea in a world where all normal values of civilised conduct have been turned upside down.

Lord Touchwood and Cynthia are marginally less trusting than Mellefont. They are inclined to have more doubts than he, but even they are swept along by the sheer brilliance of Maskwell's plotting. Both they and Mellefont are finally rescued by the twists and turns of the author's plot rather than through using their own wits. Villainy is finally brought low because it overreaches and defeats itself, while passion tears itself in tatters. When Lady Touchwood learns of Maskwell's scheme to marry Cynthia, she flies after him with a dagger. Cynthia and Lord Touchwood overhear this crucial showdown between passion and villainy and in so doing ensure the downfall of two characters who between them were intent on wrecking the ordered stability of family life.

What makes the play uncomfortable to watch is the fact that it is not rational strategy that finally overcomes villainy but the brilliant designs of the author. As a result, most of the characters are completely bewildered at the end of the play, still caught up as they are in their own intrigues and deceptions. Lord Froth wakes up from a drunken sleep to find that his wife has been stargazing with Brisk. Sir Paul Plyant, insulted by his sister, has been deserted by his wife who has been idling away the time in the garden with Careless. The main characters, Mellefont and Cynthia, can hardly credit their good fortune in escaping disaster and surviving intact. On the other hand, Lord Touchwood is left facing the complete wreck of his personal life, ruined by what he himself calls 'the viper of base treachery'.

Congreve's play revolves around the intrigues of a family, a family that was clearly meant to be seen as a microcosm of contemporary high society. The portrait was far from flattering. There is folly and deceit in plentiful measure as the various members or friends of the family pursue their selfish ends. The women, who are normally seen as the guardians of family stability, are shown in a particularly unflattering light. Even Jeremy Collier was to note in his later attack on contemporary playwrights that three of the four women characters shown in the play behave like whores. No wonder the ladies complained at Congreve's treatment of them, to which he responded in the dedication of the play.[4]

Congreve had taken great pains in *The Double Dealer* to show that society, because it was self-engrossed and populated by fools, was an easy prey for passionate plotters such as Lady Touchwood and lowly plotters such as Maskwell. Maskwell, and his accomplice Lady Touchwood, may be seen as fanciful reflections of the all too real plotter, Robert Young, who in 1692 almost succeeded in falsely branding leading figures in contemporary society as traitors to King William.[5] Congreve was concerned in his play to show how fragile civil society was and how easily it could be destroyed. His play may be read as a social and political allegory, a warning to be on guard against the enemy within. What was less clear was how best to defend the body politic. Although there was villainy and plotting, it seemed that there was little to be done about it except trust to kind fortune and the propensity of villainy to destroy itself.

The need for a rational strategy for survival was obvious but as yet Congreve had seemingly not developed a clear concept of what this might be. It was hardly reassuring to suggest to the audience as his final word that villainy was essentially self-defeating, if meanwhile Lord Touchwood was faced by the devastated wreck of his personal life and the young lovers had arguably seen enough examples of failed relationships to frighten them off marriage for ever. The problems raised by the play are literally swept off stage in the last two pages. Lady Touchwood and Maskwell are brought on in disgrace only to be swiftly dismissed with rhetorical outrage. Meanwhile the young couple about to be married are offered a serene blessing by the most cruelly betrayed and cuckolded Lord Touchwood whose own life is in pieces. This final dissonance makes for a distinctly thoughtful rather than a festive ending. It is little wonder that the play failed to please the town. In the end it was rescued not so much by its own merits but by Dryden's fulsome poem of praise in the published text and by the fact that Queen Mary ordered a command performance. At least the Royal family was astute enough to realise that the play had a political edge and that buried deep within its subtext was a warning against all obsessive plotters, whether confirmed Jacobites or merely self-seeking commoners. For most theatre-goers the political subtext was not sufficiently developed to be immediately apparent.

Congreve never took kindly to criticism and lashed out unwisely in his dedication at those who had objected to his play : 'I hear a great many of the Fools are angry at me, and I am glad of it; for I Writ at them, not to 'em.' [vol. 2, p. 12] He suppressed this comment from later editions of the play. He also ensured in future that his satire was more judicious both in form and execution, and that the political subtext of his work was more clearly defined.

LOVE FOR LOVE

The festive mood of *Love for Love* seems to herald at first sight a return to the frivolous, libertine world of *The Old Batchelour*. Even the major characters, Valentine and Angelica have something about them of a Bellmour and a Belinda, albeit a few years older and still unmarried. They are an astute pair of pleasure-seekers who have had plenty of time to sow their wild oats and both seem very far removed indeed from the sweet, almost sentimentalised young couple at the centre of *The Double Dealer*. In contrast to the virtuous Mellefont who has steadfastly resisted his aunt's advances, Valentine has managed to father several illegitimate children (making no real provision for their future) while squandering his cash in pursuit of a wealthy heiress, Angelica. In consequence, he is now deeply in debt and obliged to make a humiliating settlement with his father, resigning his right to inherit his father's estate in return for a mere £4000, which will clear his most pressing debts. Angelica, for her part, has enjoyed all the pleasures of wit and wealth and has gaily allowed Valentine to beggar himself in pursuing her, without in return giving him any tangible sign of commitment. As an astute young lady who values her good name, she has studiously avoided the lure of sexual contact. The double standard of the age made it perfectly acceptable for Valentine to have illegitimate children; but if an unmarried society heiress like Angelica were to become pregnant, her reputation would be compromised beyond repair.

The play is far less tightly structured than *The Double Dealer*. Events are spaced out over a longer period of time – two days and an intervening night rather than just a few hours – which is done to accommodate the bustle of two separate families and their intrigues. There are also two quite distinct locations, Valentine's lodgings and a room in Foresight's house. Both are scenically very simple, a simplicity that may well have been necessitated by the financial constraints facing the new actors' company in this their first production at Lincoln's Inn Fields in 1695. There are no melodramatic scenes, as in *The Double Dealer*, when violent arguments are overheard by characters concealed on a different part of the stage. However, there are theatrical 'discoveries', at the beginning and in the middle of an act, when shutters are drawn aside to reveal a character already on stage. In Act 4, Scene 1, for instance, Valentine's manservant Jeremy, 'Goes to the Scene, which opens and discovers *Valentine* upon a Couch disorderly dress'd, *Scandal* by him'. [vol. 2, p. 145] In general, however, the use of the stage is restrained and functional rather than visually significant: it is a bare space to be filled out by the actors, and does not depend on contemporary visual references. In this respect, it is closer in feel to the bare stage of the Elizabethan and Jacobean theatre than to the scenic stage of the Restoration.

The main action of the play is concerned with Valentine's attempt to make Angelica openly commit herself to him, while he simultaneously takes evasive measures to avoid having to sign the conveyance prepared by his father. His ruse is to pretend madness. This works very effectively in respect of his legal position; he obviously cannot sign a conveyance if he is not *compos mentis*. But the ploy fails in respect of Angelica as she suspects that Valentine is up to mischief and is resolved to give trick for trick. She in turn puts Valentine to the test by pretending to consider in all seriousness a marriage with Valentine's father, Sir Sampson Legend. Her ruse is far more successful than Valentine's. Faced by the degrading prospect of the loss of the woman he loves to his own father, Valentine is finally prepared to sign away any future prospect of wealth. As he himself states at the end of Act 5: 'I never valu'd Fortune, but as it was subservient to my Pleasure; and my only Pleasure was to please this Lady.' [vol. 2, p. 170] Angelica now has the proof she wants of his commitment. One brief phrase sums up her feelings, 'Generous Valentine'. At which point, she freely gives herself to Valentine, dismissing and humiliating Sir Sampson quite deliberately in the process.

Around this main plot are woven a number of subsidiary actions in the same Jonsonian manner as one finds in *The Old Batchelour*. Even some of the characters involved in these secondary actions are determined eccentrics reminiscent of Jonson's humours characters. This is in particular true of Angelica's uncle, the superstitious old Foresight who, like Fondlewife, has married a lusty young wife. Mrs Foresight spreads her affections far and wide as Fondlewife is tucked up in bed by nurse who will later in the night bring him his urinal, 'just upon the turning of the Tide'. Fondlewife is totally absorbed by his obsession with astrology and his attempts to predict the future; meanwhile, he is completely blind to what is actually happening in front of his eyes. At least, his belief in the way all events and behaviour are determined by the stars permits him to accept the fact of being a cuckold with considerable equanimity: 'Why, if I was born to be a Cuckold, there's no more to be said'. [Act 2, vol. 2, p. 116]

Another humours figure is Ben, Sir Sampson's youngest son. He is newly returned from a lengthy time at sea and is so engrossed in his world of the sea that he initially fails to recognise his own father and then proceeds to ask after his brother Dick who has been dead these two years. Ben's language is invariably salty and forthright; he can always be relied upon to

comment on events that reduce others to discreet silence. For
instance, the prospect of his father marrying Angelica provokes
him into declaring:

> Mess, I fear his Fire's little better than Tinder; may-hap it will
> only serve to light up a Match for some Body else. The Young
> Woman's a Handsom Young Woman, I can't deny it: But
> Father, if I might be your Pilot in this Case, you should not
> marry her. It's just the same thing, as if so be you should Sail so
> far as the *Streights* without Provision.
>
> [Act 5, vol. 2, p. 167]

Sir Sampson angrily orders him to be mute. Ben displays a
similar, endearing lack of tact throughout the whole play, which
provokes a number of characters to refer to him as a fish or sea-
calf. The ground is prepared for some of this later imagery even
before Ben's first entry. Valentine and his friends are discussing
the news that Ben is to marry Miss Prue, which leads Mrs Frail to
comment facetiously, 'Well, if he be but as great a Sea-Beast as
she is a Land-Monster, we shall have a most Amphibious Breed –
The Progeny will be all Otters.' [Act 1, vol. 2, p. 110]

A completely different kind of subplot involves Scandal who is
Valentine's trusty friend, much in the mould of Vainlove and
Careless. But he intervenes more directly in the action than these
two (for instance, Valentine's feigned madness is almost
certainly his idea) and he pursues his own erotic liaisons,
including one with Mrs Foresight, with as much vigour as
Valentine pursues Angelica. His affair with Mrs Foresight, in
which he sets about seducing her in front of her husband, is a
frank exploration of the pleasures and pitfalls of adultery.
Scandal duly enjoys his night with Mrs Foresight, only to find
that she denies the fact to his face the very next morning. In the
game of adultery, she is a professional: Scandal a mere amateur.
In the depiction of their relationship, with appetite finely
counterbalanced by the instinct for self-preservation, Congreve
shows a completely new maturity and security of touch. There
are superficial battles of wit in this play, as in his earlier work,
but the sparring between Scandal and Mrs Foresight reaches new
levels of daring and sophistication:

MRS FORESIGHT: O Monstrous! What are Conscience and Honour?

SCANDAL: Why, Honour is a Publick Enemy, and Conscience a Domestick Thief; and he that would secure his Pleasure, must pay a Tribute to one, and go halves with t' other. As for Honour, that you have secur'd, for you have purchas'd a perpetual Opportunity for Pleasure.

MRS FORESIGHT: An Opportunity for Pleasure!

SCANDAL: Aye, your Husband, a Husband is an Opportunity for Pleasure, so you have taken care of Honour, and 'tis the least I can do to take care of Conscience.

MRS FORESIGHT: And so you think we are free for one another?

SCANDAL: Yes, Faith, I think so; I love to speak my mind.

MRS FORESIGHT: Why then I'll speak my mind. Now as to this Affair between you and me. Here you make Love to me; why, I'll confess it does not displease me. Your Person is well enough, and your Understanding is not amiss.

SCANDAL: I have no great Opinion of my self; yet, I think, I'm neither Deform'd, nor a Fool.

MRS FORESIGHT: But you have a Villanous Character; you are a Libertine in Speech, as well as Practice.

SCANDAL: Come, I know what you would say, – you think it more dangerous to be seen in Conversation with me, than to allow some other Men the last Favour; you mistake, the Liberty I take in Talking is purely affected for the Service of your Sex. He that first cries out stop Thief, is often he that has stoln the Treasure. I am a Juggler, that act by Confederacy; and if you please, we'll put a Trick upon the world.

MRS FORESIGHT: Ay; but you are such an universal Juggler, – that I'm afraid you have a great many Confederates.

SCANDAL: Faith, I'm sound.

MRS FORESIGHT: O, fie – I'll swear you're Impudent.

SCANDAL: I'll swear you're Handsome.

MRS FORESIGHT: Pish, you'd tell me so, tho' you did not think so.

SCANDAL: And you'd think so, tho' I should not tell you so: And now I think we know one another pretty well.

[Act 3, vol. 2, pp. 139–40]

This is no mere game of wit for wit's sake, but a mutual probing, a stripping away of the social mask, to reveal the naked sexual drive beneath the fine clothes and genteel manners. Both characters are lusty in their appetites, sexually and mentally sound, and minded to commit adultery without the need for romantic trappings in terms of either language or behaviour. Scandal's wit helps them quickly to dispose of the problems of honour and conscience. At the end of this exchange, as Scandal asserts, both parties 'know one another pretty well'. All that remains is for them to implement their understanding.

In the case of Scandal and Mrs Foresight, there is a careful balance in their behaviour between appetite and self-control. However, a further group of minor characters, and the subplots in which they are involved, are used to show the dangers of completely unbridled appetite. Tattle, for instance, is totally wrapped up in a world of secret intrigues and amours. He prides himself on, and is known for, his extensive knowledge of the love-life of the town. He claims secrecy, but his vanity always pushes him towards the betraying of real or imagined secrets. Meanwhile, he pursues young flesh, in the shape of Miss Prue, and expensive flesh, in the shape of Angelica, with single-minded dedication. He is inclined to see himself as a skilled practitioner in the art of love, a man full of guile and strategy. While he finds it easy to seduce and subsequently dismiss Miss Prue, Angelica and her allies prove more than a match for him. By the end of the play, he is tricked into marrying Mrs Frail – he dressed as a friar and she as a nun – and all the while he thought his disguised marriage partner was Angelica. Tattle gets the reward he deserves: a wife who wants and values him as little as he wants and values her.

Miss Prue, Foresight's daughter from his first marriage, is a young adolescent, a novice in affairs of the heart, whose appetite for sex is as untutored as it is voracious. Despite her lack of sophistication, she prefers Tattle's erotic games to the clumsy wooing attempted by Sir Sampson's younger son, Ben, in deference to his father's wishes. However, when Tattle brusquely rejects her, she threatens to throw herself at any suitable male, including Robin the Butler. She is finally led off to be locked up by nurse, an unhappy victim of her unsated sexual drive.

In complete contrast, Mrs Frail, younger sister to Mrs Foresight, is a sophisticated society lady who is on the hunt for a wealthy husband. She is willing to consider anything that is male, has a substantial estate and is capable of saying yes. In turn she considers the whole gamut of Legend males as potential husbands: Valentine's younger brother, Ben, the unsophisticated sea-calf; the aging Sir Sampson himself; and finally Valentine in his mad state. All of these, she thinks, are males she can easily manipulate. Finally she is tricked into marriage with a man disguised as a friar whom she thinks is Valentine but who is in fact Tattle. Even then she comments to her sister, 'it's well it's no worse'. Like her sister, she is a hard-headed pragmatist who sees marriage as a passport to material comfort and unhampered, extramarital pleasure. For that purpose Tattle will serve as well as any other male who is not too swift-witted.

The addiction of this group of characters to money, status and sex makes them appear at best ridiculous and at worst grotesque. Their plots and schemes are brought to nothing, partly by their own conflicting aims, and partly by the deliberate strategies of the true wits, Valentine and Scandal, both of whom are aided and abetted by Valentine's intelligent and quick-witted manservant, Jeremy. In many ways the relationship between Jeremy and Valentine is as important as that between Scandal and Valentine. Despite the fact that theirs is a relationship based on economic inequality, there is considerable trust and affection between them. Jeremy has a natural wit and a realistic assessment of life and other people, which makes him a perfect foil to his witty but often impulsive master.

At the very heart of the play is a political debate between the values of the former age of Stuart absolutism and the new age of Whig consensual government, mirroring the debate that Locke engaged in with the Tory philosopher, Filmer, in his *First Treatise of Government*.[6] Sir Sampson Legend is an entertaining but still potentially dangerous advocate of outmoded Stuart values. During the course of the action, he attempts to impose his will on his son with absolute authority. But both Valentine and Angelica outwit him with their more sophisticated grasp of the nature of contract and through their use of deliberate strategies to counter his threat of brute economic force. Angelica in particular leads Sir Sampson a merry dance as she pretends to take seriously his proposal of marriage. He claims to be a rationalist and an opportunist who dismisses Foresight's superstitious beliefs with pithy aphorisms, such as, 'Pox o' th' time; there's no time but the time present' [Act 2, vol. 2, p. 116] or 'there never was a lucky Hour after the first opportunity' [Act 4, vol. 2, p. 148]. But his opportunism lacks a firm base of judgement or discernment, which invariably means that his actions are misconceived and misdirected. Sir Sampson is a bundle of unfocused and wasted energy.

No clue is given as to Sir Sampson's background. Some critics have assumed that he is a wealthy merchant,[7] others that he belongs to the landed squirarchy.[8] Congreve very carefully covers his tracks, presumably to avoid giving offence. Sir Sampson, as far as the play is concerned, is a representative of an older Tory generation (which makes it most unlikely that he is a wealthy merchant) who believes passionately in the traditional Stuart values of divinely ordained, absolute authority. He is equally passionately opposed to the new age which appears to value wit more than these traditional values. The whole play amounts to a damning critique of his views.

At the end of the play, Sir Sampson is unceremoniously dismissed. His expulsion from the action is as decisive and conclusive as was that of James II from the shores of England in 1688. Like the Catholic James, Sir Sampson and his values are now quite irrelevant to the sophisticated new world of London in the 1690s. Valentine and Angelica represent the new age. They can both be thoughtless and cruel; they have both indulged their appetites but they have come to respect and value each other; and when they have tested each other almost to destruction, they are both prepared to give unconditional commitment to each other. There are devious plotters and a would-be absolutist patriarch in this work, but they are brought low by the use of prudent strategy and carefully deliberated contractual agreement. This is the political agenda for the new age of Whig consensual government. The play thus can and certainly should be read as a triumphal celebration of the new personal and social values implicit in the Glorious Revolution of 1688. It was to remain Congreve's most joyous creation, having at its centre a perfect balance between festive and thoughtful comedy.

THE WAY OF THE WORLD

In place of the festive mood that pervades *Love for Love*, there is a darker hue in *The Way of the World*. In this his final play,

Congreve blends together satire and thoughtful comedy into a
dramatic whole that at times has something of the structure and
feel of a tragicomedy. Even the villains in this piece, Mr Fainall
and Mrs Marwood, are more threatening (because less melodra-
matically depicted) than Lady Touchwood and Maskwell in *The
Double Dealer*, even if they are decisively defeated at the end of
the play.

Although the play is written with the same kind of neoclassic
precision one finds in *The Double Dealer*, Congreve deliberately
abandons the unity of place in *The Way of the World*. He reverts
to earlier Restoration custom by setting Act 1 in a public
watering-place, not an inn as might have happened in the
Restoration, but a fashionable chocolate-house. Act 2 is set in
St James's Park; this too mirrors the practice of earlier Restoration playwrights who normally made use of one or more
fashionable outdoor venues in their comedies (The Mall, Hyde
Park, Mulberry Garden were all popular locations). However,
unlike earlier Restoration comedies, even the public settings are
used to concentrate attention on the major characters rather than
fill in the scene with a series of atmospheric character sketches.
Finally, the last three acts are confined to a room in Lady
Wishfort's house. Here Congreve reverts to a domestic and
family setting, complete with friends and hangers-on, reminiscent of *The Double Dealer*.

In contrast to this breach in the unity of place, there is strict
unity of time in the play. Congreve even goes as far as to state that
the time is 'equal to that of the Presentation'. This has a number
of discernible consequences. Above all it makes the action seem
very compressed, with events crowding in on each other thick and
fast. In addition, events off-stage are of necessity far too rushed.
For instance, towards the end of Act 4, Petulant leaves quite
drunk to sleep off his hangover, claiming that he is going home to
bed his maid. Not long afterwards, by the end of Act 5, he is
summoned back by Mirabell and appears on stage still rubbing
the sleep out of his eyes. In reality, he would hardly have had time
to get undressed, let alone attempt to sleep with his maid and then
fall into a drunken slumber.

Another more significant consequence of Congreve's decision
to make the time taken by the action equal that of the presentation
is that, of necessity, much of what has happened in the past has to

be revealed in the dialogue. Because of this, the action of the past at times seems to be as important as that of the present, much as it does in neoclassic tragedy.

There is also strict unity of action in the play, which is primarily concerned with tracing out the schemes of Mirabell to obtain from Mrs Millamant her unequivocal agreement to marriage, while at the same time securing the half of her fortune which is still in the control of her aunt, Lady Wishfort. All the remaining characters, and the subplots in which they are involved, revolve around Mirabell. He is central to all their doings, their loves, their hates and their aspirations. In this sense, the play is almost a monodrama.

Mirabell is the most fully worked out of all Congreve's male characters. In most of his other comedies, the male characters have tended to pale to insignificance by comparison with the strong female characters he created. Mellefont, for instance, in *The Double Dealer* is no match for his aunt Lady Touchwood and even finds the mildly promiscuous Lady Plyant a problem. Even Valentine in *Love for Love* is slower-witted and far less astute than Angelica, the woman he loves. Mirabell, however, is a consummate comic hero who seems able to control and shape the responses of others through a combination of charm and brilliant strategy. He is not without his faults. He invariably likes to have his own way and enjoys organising other people's lives; he is inclined to be sententious and pompous; he can also be devious, manipulative and at times even downright amoral in his behaviour. But he is thoughtful and sensitive, and well able to balance out enlightened self-interest with consideration for others. His conduct is informed by a clear gentlemanly code of honour, which gives him a distinct set of values and precepts by which to act himself and by which to judge the behaviour of others. Above all, he is able to restrain his appetites and to focus his desires. Having found a goal he really wishes to achieve, in this case marriage with Millamant, he is single-minded in pursuing it.

The action of the past which is explored in the play gives rise to a crucial question about Mirabell and his earlier behaviour. Why did he never marry Mrs Fainall, Lady Wishfort's daughter, when she was the affluent widow, Arabella Languish, with whom he enjoyed an extended affair? She was seemingly a perfect match: she had wealth, beauty and an even temper. They were lovers who were close to each other. Why then did he refuse to marry her and instead insist, when they both suspected she was pregnant, that she should marry Fainall, one of his less attractive acquaintances? Arabella had such confidence in Mirabell that she was even prepared, before her marriage to Fainall, to make over to Mirabell the whole of her estate in trust in order to guard against any possible ill usage on the part of Fainall. In return, Mirabell now shares with her all the secrets of his love for Millamant, including the detailed schemes he devises to get Millamant's hand and wrench her fortune out of the grasp of Lady Wishfort. Mrs Fainall thus becomes an accomplice with him in plotting against her own mother. Despite all that has happened between them, they have remained the closest of friends. Why then did he not marry her?

The answer is central to an understanding of Congreve's conception of this character. He clearly sees Mirabell, and wishes his audience to see Mirabell, as a deeply honest man who entered into a frank and mature relationship with Arabella Languish. Having explored both her character and her body in depth, he found himself in the end unable to respond with the same intensity of emotion to her as she clearly felt for him. One can only guess at the reasons, but there are hints in the text. Her mother, for instance, reveals the information that her daughter was given a strict puritanical upbringing and was taught to have an aversion for men: even her dolls were all of the female sex. Her first husband (whose name, Languish, clearly suggests a less-than-virile, masculine temperament) was chosen by Lady Wishfort. This may well have had the effect of stifling in Arabella the kind of spontaneous expression of emotion and frank sensuality that Mirabell would expect in a lover. He was perfectly prepared to enter into an honest, exploratory relationship with her, but presumably came away with sufficient doubts as to make it impossible to proceed to a marriage contract. Mirabell wants more than security and wealth from a marriage: he also wants the reciprocity of mutually given and mutually enjoyed spiritual and physical delight. Clearly he did not find this with Arabella Languish.

What is both touching and surprisingly mature about his present relationship with her is that it has not collapsed into guilt, self-pity and recrimination, but has developed into a profoundly supportive friendship. There is no doubt whatsoever that

Arabella Fainall is the loser in all this, but she accepts her defeat with quiet dignity. There is an almost Chekhovian sense of sadness about Mrs Fainall who, like a character in *The Seagull*, has to look on while the man she loves proposes to and wins the woman he loves. And she is then asked by her rival to give her approbation to their agreement:

MILLAMANT: *Fainall*, what shall I do? Shall I have him? I think I must have him.
MRS FAINALL: Ay, ay, take him, take him, what shou'd you do?
MILLAMANT: Well then – I'll take my Death I'm in a horrid Fright – *Fainall*, I shall never say it – Well – I think – I'll endure you.
MRS FAINALL: Fy, fy, have him, have him, and tell him so in plain Terms: For I am sure you have a mind to him.
MILLAMANT: Are you? I think I have – and the horrid Man looks as if he thought so too – Well, you ridiculous Thing you, I'll have you – I won't be kiss'd, nor I won't be thank'd – Here, kiss my hand tho' – So, hold your Tongue now, don't say a Word.

[Act 4, vol. 3, pp. 57–8]

Between these lines, as in a Chekhov play, there is a depth of subtextual feeling that needs all the art and skill of an accomplished actress to be communicated to an audience. While Mrs Fainall's words express support and encouragement for Mirabell and Millamant at this moment when they agree to have each other in marriage, her eyes and her voice tell a quite different and altogether more poignant story.

By comparison with Mrs Fainall, her friend Mrs Marwood is only a pale shadow of a character. She lusts after Mirabell, rather in the same manner as Lady Wishfort also lusts after him. But unlike Lady Wishfort, Mrs Marwood has found temporary consolation in the shape of her friend's husband, Mr Fainall. These two are in many ways perfectly matched and certainly deserve each other. Both are motivated by appetite, greed and envy. They claim to be passionate lovers, and indeed they do quarrel with passion. But the only thing that appears to motivate their coupling is the rush of adrenalin associated with furtive and illicit sex. (At least once they have been caught *in flagrante* by

Foible and Mincing who surprised them in the blue garret when Mrs Fainall was in Hyde Park and the two serving-women were thought to be out walking.) Significantly, the only moment when they have any physical contact on stage is when they have quarrelled violently and Fainall tries to restrain his mistress who is threatening to reveal all and create a public scandal.

The cause of their quarrel is Mrs Marwood's selfish lusting after Mirabell which makes her do all in her power to ruin his romance with Millamant. She reveals, for instance, to Lady Wishfort that Mirabell is only making advances to her in order to conceal his growing involvement with Millamant. When Mrs Marwood overhears Foible's declaration that Mirabell 'can't abide her', her desire for revenge knows no bounds. There is something pathetic about her, a decaying beauty, well past the first flush of youth, who has never yet enjoyed the open and honest affection of an unattached lover. (This poignance was doubtless not lost on the first actress who played the role and for whom Congreve wrote the part, namely Elizabeth Barry, who by 1700 was, in reality, a somewhat older version of the character she was playing.)

There is no such poignance in Fainall who comes over as a thoroughly unpleasant fortune-hunter. He married Arabella Languish for her wealth and has already, or so he thinks, wheedled her out of the best part of her fortune. (He, of course, is completely unaware that she has already made over her fortune in trust to Mirabell.) He has also persuaded Mrs Marwood to lavish her money on their mutual pleasures. Like Maskwell, he is an outsider who has no sense of family or social obligation. He pursues his own advantage, his 'desire of Power after power' with the single-minded ruthlessness of Hobbes's man in the raw state of nature. Mirabell (in contrast to Mellefont in *The Double Dealer*) is sufficiently astute to see through Fainall from the outset and accordingly uses carefully planned legal strategies to set a firm limit to his scope for manoeuvre. Even at the end of the play, there is still hope that Fainall can be tamed with the help of legally binding contracts and can be persuaded, through social and financial pressure, to return to the fold of civilisation.

Arguably the most poignant figure in the whole play is Lady Wishfort, a widow who still experiences all the desires and longings of robust sexuality but whose face and body are so decayed and damaged by the ravages of time as to repel all but false pretenders to her bed. Because she still controls half of Millamant's fortune, which can only be released when her niece marries with her consent, Mirabell has pretended to court Lady Wishfort as a means of pursuing his developing romance with Mrs Millamant. This strategy was ruined when Marwood revealed his real intentions to Lady Wishfort. Now Mirabell arranges for his own manservant, Waitwell, to personate a supposedly wealthy uncle of Mirabell's called Sir Rowland in order to lure Lady Wishfort into the embarrassing situation of a mock marriage contract. The intention is to blackmail her into releasing Millamant's money.

Lady Wishfort is constantly deceived, abused and exploited by all those around her. Marwood lies to her; her own daughter joins with Mirabell to plot against her; even Foible her personal servant, to whom she has shown great kindness, conspires against her. (Foible readily joins forces with Mirabell, in return for which he provides her with a husband, in the shape of his manservant Waitwell, and the promise of a well-stocked farm.) Why is it that all conspire against Lady Wishfort? The answer is distressingly simple. Her responses to people and situations are so fundamentally dishonest and hypocritical that no one can take her seriously. Although she herself is prone to lustful sexual longings, she does everything in her power to bring her daughter up to be a puritan prude. One moment she dreams of being tumbled on the couch by a rampant Sir Rowland, the next she talks of withdrawing from the world and playing innocent shepherdesses with her friend and confidante, Marwood. Totally devoid of judgement, it is hardly surprising that no one deals honestly with her. Even her choice of reading matter is a deliberate sham: a collection of puritan texts designed to impress the casual visitor. Congreve had his revenge on Jeremy Collier by making Lady Wishfort the proud possessor, amongst other texts, of Collier's *Short View*: meanwhile the bottle of liqueur is hidden under her dressing-table and she is made up and dressed to meet a new lover who, she hopes, will be forward and brisk. So much for the integrity of non-juring, High Church prudes. Lady Wishfort represented a barbed satirical portrait of the average Collier supporter at the turn of the century. Although this was not likely to endear Congreve to the ladies of the town (who were generally inclined to favour Collier), he was careful to avoid deliberate malice in his satire and left sufficient room for genuine human sympathy for this old peeled wall of a woman.

The same endearing warmth and sympathy are shown by Congreve towards the minor characters in the play. Sir Wilful Witwoud, for instance, Lady Wishfort's nephew, is a warm-hearted country bumpkin rather than an embarrassingly plain speaking sea-calf like Ben in *Love for Love*. He is teased at first mercilessly by his half-brother, the fop, Witwoud. Later he manages to disgrace himself by becoming embarrassingly drunk at the very moment when his aunt expects him to pay his court to Millamant. But eventually he proves to be a natural ally to Mirabell and Millamant in their struggles against Lady Wishfort. Briefed off-stage by Mirabell, he gladly pretends that he is willing to marry Millamant in deference to his aunt's wishes, in order to ensure that Millamant does not forfeit the half of her fortune controlled by Lady Wishfort. In the final scene of the play, he also emerges as a character of surprising strength and firmness. When Fainall, in the closing moments of the action, threatens to draw his sword against his own wife, it is Sir Wilful who at once steps forward to prevent him and instructs him to make his '*Bear-Garden* flourish somewhere else'.

The socialites Witwoud and Petulant are far more attractive versions of the Froths, the Brisks and the Tattles seen in Congreve's earlier comedies. They may be vacuous fops, but they are also given enough genuine human traits to make them seem diverting and amusing companions. Witwoud, in particular, has an entertaining facility with words and has at the ready a seemingly endless stock of resonant phrases or similes to describe both events and people, especially his friend Petulant. In Act 1, for instance, he paints an amusingly satiric portrait of Petulant before his first entry:

> Petulant's my Friend, and a very honest Fellow, and a very pretty Fellow, and has a smattering – Faith and Troth a pretty deal of an odd sort of a small Wit: Nay, I'll do him Justice. I'm his Friend, I won't wrong him. – And if he had any Judgment in the World, – he wou'd not be altogether contemptible. Come, come, don't detract from the Merits of my Friend.
>
> [Act 1, vol. 3, pp. 20–1]

In Act 4, he is greatly entertained by Petulant's drunken dispute with Sir Wilful, which he describes with an appropriately witty simile:

> That's the Jest; there was no Dispute. They cou'd neither of 'em speak for Rage, and so fell a splutt'ring at one another like two roasting Apples.
>
> [Act 4, vol. 3, p. 58]

A few moments later, he encourages his drunken friend to go home to bed, using the same combination of warmth and disparagement that we saw in Act 1:

> Do, wrap thy self up like a *Wood-louse*, and dream Revenge – And hear me, if thou canst learn to write by To-morrow Morning, Pen me a Challenge – I'll carry it for thee.
>
> [Act 4, vol. 3, p. 59]

None of this has the sparkle and vigour of true wit; it is too domestic, too close to everyday experience. But that is also the source of its strength. Underpinning Witwoud's gentle barbs, there is a warm and tolerant acceptance of his friend's short-comings and follies.

Significantly, both Witwoud and Petulant have weaknesses from which they are seen to hide behind their gaudy masks. Witwoud is ashamed of his past, when his half-brother would have made him prentice to a felt-maker in Shrewsbury; although he escaped to London, the only employment he managed to find for himself was as a lowly attorney's clerk. These aspects of his past he prefers to keep well hidden. Petulant for his part feels so insignificant that he even pays people to call for him in public places. He would dearly love to court a fine lady like Millamant, but can never find the right words. He hides from his inadequacies in drunken verbal fisticuffs and then goes home to sleep with his maid, who is presumably the only woman who takes him seriously because she is economically dependent on him.

These various characters represent much refined versions of figures seen in earlier Congreve plays. What is quite new in *The Way of the World* is the depiction of the relationship between Mirabell and Mrs Millamant (we are never told her first name).

These two are exquisitely well matched. She, witty, intelligent,
extremely well-read and wealthy (even with only half her fortune
in her possession). He, equally intelligent and well-read, is
somewhat less wealthy but instead has a plentiful supply of
charm and astute foresight. Even before the play begins, there is a
clear understanding between these two that they want to marry,
although they have yet to establish in some detail what marriage
will entail for their personal lives. They are also both keen that
they should obtain the remainder of Millamant's fortune (some
£6000) in Lady Wishfort's possession so that they may live
completely secure from the financial hazards and vicissitudes of
city life. (Congreve was himself only too painfully aware at the
time how financial pressures could constrain an individual's
personal life.)

When one analyses the way Mirabell and Millamant respond to
each other, one notices that Mirabell inclines to be patronising
and somewhat sententious in the way he talks to Millamant. She
adopts a deliberately provocative frivolity in response and takes
delight in keeping him guessing. Finally, however, they agree to
have each other for better or worse. Their contract scene in Act 4
is a masterpiece that sets out the parameters for an ideal marriage
in Congreve's eyes, one in which the actuality of personal
commitment is perfectly balanced by the need for personal space
and personal freedom. Given the dominant position that men
enjoyed in what was still a largely patriarchal society, it is not
surprising that Millamant's demands are the most advanced:

> Trifles, – As Liberty to pay and receive Visits to and from
> whom I please; to write and receive Letters, without Inter-
> rogatories or wry Faces on your part; to wear what I please; and
> choose Conversation with regard only to my own Taste; to have
> no Obligation upon me to converse with Wits that I don't like,
> because they are your Acquaintance; or to be intimate with
> Fools, because they may be your Relations. Come to Dinner
> when I please; dine in my Dressing-room when I'm out of
> Humour, without giving a Reason. To have my Closet
> inviolate; to be sole Empress of my Tea-Table, which you
> must never presume to approach without first asking leave.
> And, lastly, where-ever I am, you shall always knock at the
> Door before you come in. These Articles subscrib'd, if I

continue to endure you a little longer, I may by degrees
dwindle into a Wife.

[Act 4, vol. 3, p. 56]

Millamant's aim in making these demands is to safeguard her
personal liberty within a framework of marital, contractual
commitment. She is no longer being frivolous, nor is she
attempting simply to score off Mirabell. There is no sparring
here for its own sake, no witty jousting for position; instead a
sparkling framework of wit is used to express very precisely the
terms and conditions under which Millamant is prepared to share
her life with Mirabell. This was a completely new conception of
wit that brought it right up against the demands of real life.
Congreve was breaking new ground here and he knew it.

In response, Mirabell is moved to comment to Millamant that
her 'Bill of Fare is something advanc'd in this latter Account'.
His view is shared by at least one modern American critic,
Maximillian Novak, who, in his study of Congreve's work,
labelled Millamant's demands 'unreasonable'.[9] Clearly even
today there are problems involved in the acceptance of such
provisos as the basis for a marriage contract in what is still largely
a male-dominated world.

When Mirabell goes on to outline his provisos, they are
essentially a patronising attempt on his part to retain some
patriarchal status in the light of Millamant's demands:

Mirabell: [. . .] *Imprimis* then, I covenant that your Acquaintance be general; that you admit no sworn Confident, or
Intimate of your own Sex; no she Friend to skreen her Affairs
under your Countenance, and tempt you to make a trial of a
mutual Secrecy. No Decoy-duck to wheedle you a *fop* –
scrambling to the Play in a Mask – Then bring you home in a
pretended Fright, when you think you shall be found out- And
rail at me for missing the Play, and disappointing the Frolick
which you had to pick me up and prove my Constancy.
MILLAMANT: Detestable *Imprimis!* I go to the Play in a Mask!
MIRABELL: *Item*, I article that you continue to like your own
Face, as long as I shall: And while it passes current with me,
that you endeavour not to new Coin it. To which end,
together with all Vizards for the Day, I prohibit all Masks

for the Night, made of Oil'd-skins, and I know not what –
Hog's Bones, Hare's Gall, Pig Water, and the Marrow of a
roasted Cat. In short, I forbid all Commerce with the
Gentlewoman in *what-d'ye-call-it* Court. *Item*, I shut my
Doors against all Bawds with Baskets, and Penny-worths of
Muslin, China, Fans, Atlasses, etc – *Item*, when you shall be
Breeding –
MILLAMANT: Ah! name it not.
MIRABELL: Which may be presum'd, with a Blessing on our
Endeavours –
MILLAMANT: Odious Endeavours!
MIRABELL: I denounce against all strait Laceing, squeezing for a
Shape, 'till you mold my Boy's Head like a Sugar-loaf; and
instead of a Man-child, make me Father to a Crooked-billet.
Lastly, to the Dominion of the *Tea Table* I submit. – But
with *proviso*, that you exceed not in your Province; but
restrain your self to native and simple *Tea Table* Drinks, as
Tea, Chocolate, and *Coffee*. As likewise to Genuine and
Authoriz'd *Tea Table* Talk – Such as mending of Fashions,
spoiling Reputations, railing at absent Friends, and so forth –
But that on no Account you encroach upon the Mens
Prerogative, and presume to drink Healths, or toast Fel-
lows; for prevention of which I banish all *Foreign Forces*, all
Auxiliaries to the *Tea Table*, as *Orange-Brandy*, all
Anniseed, Cinnamon, Citron and *Barbado's Waters*, toge-
ther with *Ratafia* and the most noble spirit of *Clary*. – But
for *Couslip-Wine, Poppy-Water*, and all *Dormitives*, those I
allow. – These *Proviso's* admitted, in other things I may
prove a tractable and complying Husband.
MILLAMENT: O, horrid *Proviso's*! filthy Strong-waters! I toast
Fellows! Odious Men! I hate your odious Proviso's.
                                              [Act 4, vol. 3, pp. 56–7]

Certain of these provisos show Mirabell attempting to constrain
some of the freedoms Millamant has demanded. All of them show
him at his most sententious and pompous, and Millamant is quite
justified in making her brief mocking responses. Mirabell is very
keen to establish that he is the one who will still determine and
control the parameters of their everyday lives; he will allow
certain concessions but not others. More important than any of his

domestic provisos, however, is the simple fact that in general, and despite his reservations, he agrees to hers. Although he mutters about straight-lacing, and pennyworth's of muslin and drinking healths and toasting fellows, he is merely saving face. In assenting to Millamant's provisos, Mirabell has actually agreed to renounce most of the accepted signs of patriarchal control over his wife and has promised to allow her instead the considerable measure of freedom she demands to be herself within the confines of marriage. Here too Congreve was breaking new ground.

By the end of the play, this private contract between two consenting adults is given public approval. Fainall, who has learnt of his wife's former affair with Mirabell, threatens a public scandal unless Lady Wishfort agrees to give him control of his wife's and Millamant's fortune. Mirabell proves more than a match for Fainall by producing for all to see the legal conveyance whereby Mrs Fainall, before her marriage to Fainall, made over to Mirabell the whole of her estate in trust. For her part, Mrs Fainall stoutly refutes her husband's claims; lying urbanely, she denies any carnal knowledge of Mirabell. In turn she counterattacks by proving, with the testimony of Foible and Mincing, that Fainall and Marwood have committed adultery together. Fainall's plans and aspirations are dashed; both he and Marwood flee the stage in confusion. In gratitude, Lady Wishfort agrees to hand over the remainder of Millamant's fortune in her control so that Mirabell may marry her niece. The two of them are naturally delighted. Only the depth of their affection worries them: to be so in love is to be vulnerable. But that is a risk they must take and both of them agree to do so. Mirabell concludes the play by handing back to Arabella, his one-time lover, her deed of trust in the hope that 'It may be a Means, well manag'd, to make you live easily together'. [Act 5, vol. 3, p. 77]

Like *Love for Love*, *The Way of the World* is a profoundly political play. Once again the values of the Stuart cavaliers are derided. Fainall, the fortune-hunter, who would have been treated as a swashbuckling hero in Restoration comedy, is for Congreve a despicably selfish coward whose only manly gesture is to threaten his own wife with his sword. Indeed one may see just how far Congreve has travelled from the cavalier world of Restoration playwrights by comparing Fainall with Willmore from Aphra Behn's, play *The Rover*.

One of the fascinating paradoxes of literary history is that Aphra Behn, England's first professional woman playwright, was a passionate supporter of Stuart absolutism and something of an apologist for cavalier attitudes towards women. She shows Willmore behaving completely irresponsibly towards women throughout *The Rover*, as he attempts to penetrate, by force if need be, any woman who happens to cross his path; despite this, he is rewarded at the end of the play with marriage to Helena, an attractive and spirited young woman who has just fled the convent. By the time Congreve came to write his play, Willmore has lost his attractive sides and has become Fainall, a mean-spirited, selfish fornicator who needs to be and is taught a painful lesson in civilised behaviour.

In the new world of Whig consensual government, there are civil and personal contracts at the heart of all civilised conduct. As a carefully thought-through comedy of contract, *The Way of the World* is intended to demonstrate how, despite all the vicissitudes of an unstable world in which people can and do fall a prey to their fantasies, their emotions and unbridled appetites, the wise build a stable future through mutually given and accepted consent. Patterns of interaction at a personal and family level are presented in the play as ciphers in microcosm for the macro-relationships involved in government. Individuals, like governments need to have clear objectives and clear strategies for achieving their objectives: they must expect and anticipate opposition, but if they plan wisely, they can outwit their enemies. Even when one set of plans goes awry, it is important to have a fall-back position clearly formulated in advance. And binding all things together is the security implied by a consensually based legal framework for personal and social interaction. This was Congreve's profoundly political message to his countrymen, and it represented in essence the kind of thinking that had led to the brilliantly executed Whig coup which ousted King James in 1688. Undaunted, perhaps even provoked, by Jeremy Collier's Jacobite-inspired attack on him in his *Short View*, Congreve wrote what was his most thoughtful defence of Whig ideas in *The Way of the World*.

In his four comedies, Congreve explores the nature and consequences of human appetite from a series of changing perspectives. In his earliest work, he shows a largely youthful and festive perspective on the world of appetite; gradually he becomes increasingly concerned with exploring how the harmful effects of appetite can be countered by rational strategies and contractually based order. At times social stability and order are threatened by the excessive greed or envy of one or more characters. Invariably they are defeated, sometimes because of their own uncontrolled passions and sometimes because others make wise provision to limit their freedom of action. Other characters plan a future life together in which they aim to reconcile the often conflicting demands of appetite and commitment. In his final play, Mirabell and Millamant represent the best that can be achieved in this respect. They both know and understand the problematic ways of the world, but they are both able to envisage a stable future life together based on a profound regard for each other's freedom. The respect that they show each other and the consent that they give each other represent for Congreve a personal and political ideal. In his mature work, there is no room for the politics of greed and envy, malice and tyranny. The vision he offers is one of personal and social stability, based on mature deliberation and freely given consent. For him that is the only law that can govern our personal and public lives. In establishing such a clear link between the personal and the political in his comedies, Congreve not only helped to prepare the ground for the more overtly political plays of the 1720s, but arguably foreshadowed in his work the approach that would be taken by social writers such as Ibsen almost two centuries later.

7
Tragedy, Masque and Opera

The actions of Congreve's tragedy, *The Mourning Bride*, his masque, *The Judgement of Paris*, and his opera, *Semele*, all take place in an idealised world, either the world of romantic fiction or that of classical myth. However, the author's underlying concern with the destructive power of appetite remains the same as in the comedies: what differs is the treatment. In these three works, Congreve is able to explore certain key values informing human behaviour in an abstract and highly stylised manner. Values such as loyalty, steadfastness, love, commitment, betrayal, tyranny, greed, appetite had already underpinned the responses of the characters in his comedies: here they are shown in their pristine state, effectively unencumbered by any detailed character-drawing.

THE MOURNING BRIDE

The action of *The Mourning Bride* is set in Granada, which was probably intended as a deliberate and affectionate reference to the setting of Dryden's famous heroic play, *The Conquest of Granada*. (Dryden was of course Congreve's poetic mentor and champion at the time.) In reality, however, the setting is purely abstract: there is no reference in the stage directions to any of the architectural splendours of Granada. All that is required is a room of state, a prison, and a gloomy mausoleum.

Unlike earlier Restoration tragedies, which were structured around a series of conflicts between love and honour, Congreve's play is essentially static. He seems more concerned with exploring states of mind and with painting atmospheric pictures than with showing the development of character or action. Indeed, none of his characters develop significantly during the play. Their responses are fixed from the outset, which means that they react to events in a completely predictable manner. This gives many of the speeches an aria-like quality that is reminiscent of libretto composition. It is therefore hardly surprising that the play not only opens with soft music but contains an extended reference to the power of music in the very first lines of dialogue:

> Musick has Charms to sooth a savage Breast,
> To soften Rocks, or bend a knotted Oak.
> I've read, that things inanimate have mov'd,
> And, as with living Souls, have been inform'd,
> By Magick Numbers and persuasive Sound.
> What then am I? Am I more senseless grown
> Than Trees, or Flint? O force of constant Woe!
> 'Tis not in Harmony to calm my Griefs.
> [Act 1, vol. 2, p. 185]

The action of the play revolves around the misfortunes of Almeria, the mourning bride of the title. Like Almahide, the heroine of Dryden's *Conquest of Granada*, Almeria embodies rational restraint in a world seemingly dominated by brute appetite and passion. But she is noticeably more passive than Almahide. Loyal, steadfast and grieving, she is not an active participant in events. Instead she is caught up in the conflicts engendered by her father, Manuel, King of Granada, notably his lengthy war with Anselmo, King of Valentia. Throughout she is the essentially innocent victim of others' passions.

Following a period of captivity in Valentia, when she was treated more like a visiting princess than a royal prisoner, Almeria has in secret wedded Alphonso, son of Anselmo, the King of

Valentia. The resumption of war between Granada and Valentia
has brought a ruinous reversal of fortune to the house of Valentia.
King Anselmo of Valentia is captured and subsequently perishes
in King Manuel's dungeons. Meanwhile, Anselmo's son, Alphonso, has fled with Almeria but their boat founders off the coast of
Africa (just after their hasty marriage service on board) and each
presumes the other dead.

When the action of the play opens, Almeria is grieving the loss
of her newly wedded husband, Alphonso, as well as the death of
her gentle father-in-law, King Anselmo. Her distress is heightened by the prospect of shortly having to wed one of her father's
young protégés, Garcia, the valiant son of Gonsalez who is King
Manuel's closest adviser.

King Manuel has fought yet another successful war, this time
against the Moors, and has captured the Moorish Queen, Zara,
along with her captain of horse, Osmyn. King Manuel is
immediately attracted to Zara but suspects some kind of relationship between her and Osmyn. His suspicions prove correct in
respect of Zara who is completely obsessed with Osmyn; but it
transpires that Osmyn is in fact Prince Alphonso in disguise, the
lost and much lamented husband of Almeria.

The whole of Act 2 is pervaded by a sense of Gothic gloom and
foreboding, first suggested by Almeria in a speech at the
beginning of the act:

> No, all is hush'd, and still as Death – 'Tis dreadful!
> How rev'rend is the Face of this tall Pile,
> Whose ancient Pillars rear their Marble Heads,
> To bear aloft its arch'd and pond'rous Roof,
> By its own Weight made stedfast and immoveable,
> Looking Tranquility. It strikes an Awe
> And Terror on my aking Sight; the Tombs
> And Monumental Caves of Death look Cold,
> And shoot a Chilness to my trembling Heart.
>   [Act 2, vol. 2, p. 197]

Although Alphonso and Almeria eventually find each other
near the tomb of King Anselmo, their happy reunion proves all
too short-lived and only serves to occasion a further series of
calamitous reversals. Zara comes looking for Osmyn in the

mausoleum and is provoked into a jealous frenzy by his coolness towards her. Having wormed her way into the confidence of King Manuel, Zara has authority, and uses it, to have Osmyn led away in chains. Act 3 is set in a prison and concludes even more catastrophically than Act 2. Zara has observed Almeria visiting Osmyn in prison and as a result is reduced, by the end of the act, to a paroxysm of jealous rage:

> Yes, thou shalt know, spite of thy past Distress,
> And all those Ills which thou so long hast mourn'd;
> Heav'n has no Rage, like Love to Hatred turn'd,
> Nor Hell a Fury, like a Woman scorn'd.
>
> [Act 3, vol. 2, p. 218]

Her anguish is, however, no worse than that already experienced by Osmyn/Alphonso at the thought of his bride being forcibly wedded to Garcia:

> Then *Garcia* shall lie panting on thy Bosom,
> Luxurious, revelling amidst thy Charms;
> And thou perforce must yield, and aid his Transport.
> Hell! Hell! have I not Cause to rage and rave?
> What are all Racks, and Wheels, and Whips to this?
>
> [Act 3, vol. 2, p. 216]

This powerful image of Garcia revelling amidst Almeria's charms gravely offended Jeremy Collier's prudish sensibilities. In his *Defence of the Short View* (1698) he commented that he was not even willing to cite the words of this speech because he was, 'not willing to furnish the Reader with a Collection of Indecencies'.[1]

The remaining two acts of the play are packed with melodramatic events. Act 4 revolves mainly around plans for Osmyn's execution. Zara, repenting of her jealous rage, persuades King Manuel to give Osmyn into her custody, ostensibly so as to permit her mutes to carry out the execution (she claims there are rumours of disloyalty amongst Manuel's troops), but in reality to save his life. Even Almeria, Manuel's own daughter, much to her father's displeasure, pleads on her knees for Osmyn's life. In her

distraction Almeria also reveals to Gonsalez that Osmyn is in fact
Alphonso and that they are wedded. This provokes Gonsalez into
considering how best to safeguard the future marriage of his son,
Garcia, with Almeria, and he concludes that he can only achieve
this by murdering Osmyn/Alphonso.

Act 5 is full of chaos and confusion. Against the background of
a growing rebellion against his rule, a rebellion in which even his
own daughter is implicated, King Manuel is increasingly
obsessed with his unrequited love for Zara. She, in despair at
her impossible plight, has resolved to kill both herself and Osmyn
with two bowls of poison. Unknown to her, Osmyn/Alphonso has
meanwhile already escaped from prison to join the rebellion
against King Manuel. Manuel plots to take revenge on Zara by
dressing in Osmyn's clothes, in order to confront her with her
unfaithfulness before dispatching her. He lies down to wait on the
prison floor where Osmyn was previously fettered. At this
juncture, Gonsalez enters the prison to kill Osmyn and by
mistake kills his own master, King Manuel. In order to prevent
this dire news reaching the troops, one of Gonsalez's officers cuts
off the king's head and hides it. Next Zara enters and kills herself,
having mistakenly assumed that the headless corpse confronting
her is that of Osmyn. Finally, Almeria enters and, in her distress
at seemingly finding the corpse of her husband, is about to drink
the remaining bowl of poison when she notices that the corpse is
headless. The shock causes her to drop the bowl of poison, at
which point the victorious rebels, led by Osmyn/Alphonso, enter
the prison. He is reunited with his beloved Almeria, awakening
her to a new life, and comments briefly on the way they have
been preserved through the benevolent workings of divine
providence: ɪ

> O *Garcia!* –
> Whose Virtue has renounc'd thy Father's Crimes,
> Seest thou, how just the Hand of Heav'n has been?
> Let us that thro' our Innocence survive,
> Still in the Paths of Honour persevere,
> And not from past or present Ills Despair:
> For Blessings ever wait on vertuous Deeds;
> And tho' a late, a sure Reward succeeds.
>
> [Act 5, vol. 2, p. 240]

This is not the stuff of history, either real or imagined. It is a poetic abstraction, designed, as Congreve himself spelled out in his dedication, 'to recommend and to encourage Vertue'. The action is no more than a convenient vehicle for the depiction of pure emotional states, unhampered by the normal laws and limitations of human intercourse. Every emotion is heightened to its quintessence. There is grief and suffering; there is loyalty and devotion even beyond the grave; there is erotic love of the purest kind, as yet untainted by any actual physical contact. In complete contrast, there is brute sexual appetite and the jealous passion it engenders; there is lust for absolute power and the corruption that follows from its exercise; there is physical cruelty and devious strategy; there is also murderous greed and excess. In the end, the play celebrates the victory of innocent and selfless love over the chaos engendered by destructive and brutish appetite. The whole action is seen to be encompassed within the protective embrace of divine providence. Clearly this was a play written to please the increasingly romantic taste of the ladies in the London of the 1690s; and in this Congreve succeeded admirably. *The Mourning Bride* was widely regarded by his contemporaries as his finest work.

Despite the stylistic differences, there are parallels between *The Mourning Bride* and some of Congreve's comedies. In particular, certain characters reappear as exaggerated versions of figures already seen in the comedies. Queen Zara, for instance, seems like a grossly inflated version of Lady Touchwood from *The Double Dealer*. Having failed to rouse any passion in her nephew, Mellefont, Lady Touchwood subsequently does all in her power to harm and hinder him. Likewise, Zara, obsessed with Osmyn the object of her lust, is determined, if she cannot have him, to hound and harry him even to his death. By the same token, Osmyn and Almeria are reminiscent of Mellefont and Cynthia from *The Double Dealer*; both are too kind and passive to match the energy and inventiveness of the characters ranged against them. Although Osmyn does indeed join the rebels at the end of the play, it is a matter of pure luck that he is able to do so. His flight from prison is facilitated, not by his own strategy, but by the intervention of Perez, the Captain of the Guard, who fortuitously happens to be incensed that King Manuel unjustly reproached and even struck him in public. As in *The Double Dealer*, the villains in

The Mourning Bride are brought low, not by the active opposition of the characters representing positive values, but essentially by their own excessive passions and by their evil deeds.

King Manuel is an equally inflated version of a figure from another of Congreve's comedies, namely Sir Sampson Legend from *Love for Love*. Like Sir Sampson, he expects absolute loyalty and obedience from those around him, however unreasonable his demands may be. As a result, he provokes even his own family to plot and to rebel against him. In *Love for Love*, there was a distinct political subtext to this rebellion: in *The Mourning Bride* the political subtext has become context and is made quite explicit.

In Congreve's comedies, Locke's ideas on consent as the basis of good government inform the substance and even the detailed particulars of the relationships he depicts. In *The Mourning Bride*, the ideological debate is no longer engaged at a subtextual level but is deliberately placed in the foreground. Less than ten years after the Glorious Revolution of 1688, a London audience in 1697 would need no prompting to recognise in the figure of King Manuel an exaggerated and contemptuous portrait of the deposed King James II. Hysterical, tyrannical, and demanding absolute loyalty from his creatures, Manuel, like James, only succeeds in fomenting civil discord and rebellion. Like James, he is particularly outraged at the fact that his own daughter joins the rebellion against him, which is led by his son-in-law. The parallel with James II's daughter Mary who actively encouraged and supported her husband, William of Orange, in his invasion of England was clear for all to see. But in case anyone had missed the obvious parallel, Congreve underlined it by dedicating his play to no less a person than Princess Anne, James II's younger daughter, who had likewise joined the rebellion against her father. As Congreve coyly commented in his dedication:

For they who are at that distance from Original Greatness, as to be depriv'd of the Happiness of Contemplating the Perfections and real Excellencies of Your Royal Highness's Person in Your Court, may yet behold some small Sketches and Imagings of the Vertues of Your Mind, abstracted, and represented in the Theatre.

[vol. 2, p. 180]

The virtuous and long-suffering Almeria was therefore to be · viewed as, in essence, an image of the Princess Anne. It will be clear from this that *The Mourning Bride* was more than a simple, romantic play written to please the ladies. It was above all a play intended to celebrate the virtue and honour of two royal princesses, who had had the courage to rebel against their tyrannical father and thus to ensure the future prosperity of their country and its citizens. It was an obvious political allegory, an open act of homage to two royal ladies who both became Queens of England.

Not surprisingly, given the political temper of the age, *The Mourning Bride* proved to be an enormous success. What is rather more surprising is that it continued to prove a popular play throughout most of the eighteenth century. Even Dr Johnson compared some passages in it favourably with Shakespeare. Set alongside Congreve's comedies, it is a play of no real depth or substance: it is too abstract and too rarefied. When the immediate political relevance is discounted, it seems a distinctly superficial piece. However, Dr Johnson's enthusiasm for the night scene in Act 2 provides some clue as to why *The Mourning Bride* remained a popular play. He singles out Almeria's speech describing the house of the dead for particular praise, commenting that it 'was the finest poetical passage he had ever read'.[2] In writing this scene of Gothic foreboding, Congreve had clearly anticipated the pre-romantic fascination with the medieval past that was to become increasingly marked in the late eighteenth century. In addition, the play has an operatic feel to it that obviously suited the stylised tragic acting of the early eighteenth century. It is written almost as if it were intended to be sung, and reads more like a melodramatic opera libretto than a straightforward play text. In his one and only heroic tragedy, Congreve was clearly moving towards a musical conception of poetic drama. It is therefore not at all fortuitous that he should conclude his career as a writer by creating texts to be set to music.

THE JUDGEMENT OF PARIS

Several Persons of Quality having, for the Encouragement of Musick advanced 200 Guineas, to be distributed in 4 Prizes, the

First of 100, the Second of 50, the Third of 30, and the Fourth of 20 Guineas to such Masters as shall be adjudged to compose the best; This is therefore to give Notice, That those who intend to put in for the Prizes, are to repair to Jacob Tonson at Grays-Inn-Gate before Easter next Day, where they may be further informed.

(*London Gazette*, 18–21 March 1700)

Congreve was commissioned to provide the libretto for this glittering social occasion, which was to be the talk of London in 1701. Four leading composers (John Eccles, Daniel Purcell, John Weldon and Gottfried Finger) submitted settings of Congreve's text and each was performed on a separate occasion before the final day of the competition when all four versions were performed together. The young John Weldon, organist at New College Oxford was adjudicated the winner. Congreve, in a letter to his friend, Joseph Keally, wrote a graphic description of the first of the four separate performances given in the Dorset Garden theatre on 21 March 1701:

The number of performers, besides the verse-singers, was 85. The front of the stage was all built into a concave with deal boards; all which was faced with tin, to increase and throw forwards the sound. It was all hung with sconces of wax-candles, besides the common branches of lights usual in the play-houses. The boxes and pit were all thrown into one; so that all sat in common: and the whole was crammed with beauties and beaux, not one scrub being admitted. The place where formerly the music used to play, between the pit and the stage, was turned into White's chocolate-house; the whole family being transplanted thither with chocolate, cool'd drinks, ratafia, Pontacq, &c. which ever body that would called for, the whole expence of every thing being defrayed by the subscribers. I think truly the whole thing better worth coming to see than the jubilee. And so I remain yours,

W. Congreve

Our friend Venus performed to a miracle; so did Mrs Hodgson Juno. Mrs Boman was not quite so well approved in Pallas.[3]

These performances were festive occasions that gave great delight to all concerned, except the unfortunate Moravian composer, Gottfried Finger, who came fourth in the competition. Such was his embarrassment that he quit England for the Continent and complained bitterly of the partiality of the judges.[4]

In treating the myth of the Judgement of Paris, Congreve followed the advice Dryden had given on the writing of opera librettos (in his introduction to *Albion and Albanius*) and made his text above all pleasing to the ear. It was full of resonant consonants and full-throated, vowel-based rhymes at the end of each line. His libretto was clearly a delight to set to music and equally a delight to sing. It was structured in three distinct sections, each of which culminates in an ensemble or chorus. The first section shows Mercury descending from the Heavens to the shepherd, Paris, to inform him that Jove wishes him to determine which of the three Goddesses – Juno, Pallas, or Venus – should win the golden apple for her matchless beauty. In the second section, the three Goddesses descend and vie directly with each other. In the final and longest section, each Goddess in turn is allowed to present herself to Paris and to bribe him with promises of favours. Juno offers him temporal power and urges him to let ambition fire his mind. Pallas offers him prowess at war and the laurels of victory. Venus, however, offers him the delights of love and promises, if he gives her the apple, that he shall have Helen to be his wife. Paris, unable to resist this blandishment, and also unable to tolerate any longer the darts of Venus's eyes, gives her the apple. The piece ends with a radiant final chorus celebrating the triumph of the Goddess of Love.

Congreve and the select audience viewing the masque knew full well that, in accepting Venus's offer, Paris was opting for a course of action that would lead to the rape of Menelaus's wife Helen, which would in turn provoke the protracted Trojan war. Paris may have chosen the soft delights of Venus, but his choice would lead to a war in which the gifts of Juno's statecraft and Pallas's prowess at arms would both be needed. He himself would perish during the war and the city of Troy would eventually be razed to the ground.

All of this is deliberately glossed over in Congreve's delightfully ironic treatment of the theme. For once the snares of appetite are freely indulged in. Paris cheekily instructs the Goddesses to

undress and appear naked before him, so that he may properly
judge their beauty:

> Apart let me view then each heav'nly Fair,
> For three at time there's no Mortal can bear;
> And since a gay Robe an ill Shape may disguise,
>   When each is undrest
>   I'll judge of the best,
> For 'tis not a Face that must carry the Prize.
>
> [vol. 3, p. 83]

(There is no suggestion that the actresses actually did disrobe in
performance; presumably, as in the 1989 Prom performance, they
merely discarded a symbolic piece of their attire.) Having viewed
them in all their glory and listened to their bribes, Paris rejects the
political and military prowess offered him by respectively Juno
and Pallas in favour of Venus's double-edged promise. He shall
have Helen, the fairest woman on earth, to be his, even though she
is already married to King Menelaus. As Paris awards the apple to
Venus, he begs her to stop ravishing his soul:

> I yield, I yield, O take the Prize,
> And cease, O cease, th' inchanting Song;
> All Love's Darts are in thy Eyes,
> And Harmony falls from thy Tongue.
> Forbear, O Goddess of Desire,
> Thus my ravish'd Soul to move;
> Forbear to fan the raging Fire,
> And be propitious to my Love.
>
> [vol. 3, p. 85]

There was of course a personal edge to these lines, written by
Congreve for Anne Bracegirdle; a wry plea for mercy and for
deliverance from the unbearable raging fires of love she kindled
in him.

Congreve's measured ironic stance in treating the theme is
dependent upon his audience knowing the dire consequences of
Paris's judgement. As the final chorus celebrates Venus's
decisive victory, the certain knowledge of the lengthy war that
will follow from this victory adds a special poignance to

Congreve's delightful artistic conceit. The effect is like a moment of beauty frozen in time before the ravages of war, death and destruction take over. For Congreve, there is no such thing as an innocent choice. Paris makes his choice, but in succumbing to the delights of erotic love offered by Venus, he will live to rue the day.

SEMELE

I love and am lov'd, yet more I desire;
Ah, how foolish a Thing is Fruition!
As one Passion cools, some other takes Fire,
And I'm still in a longing Condition.
    Whate'er I possess
    Soon seems an Excess.
For something untry'd I petition;
    Tho' daily I prove
    The Pleasures of love,
I die for the Joys of Ambition.
                [Act 3, Scene 2, vol. 3, p. 104]

In his final work written for the stage, his opera libretto, *Semele*, Congreve returned yet again to the theme that had preoccupied him throughout his playwriting career: namely, the destructive power of appetite and the associated dangers of ambition.

On this occasion, the theme is explored within the context of the myth of Semele and Jupiter, a myth concerned with the tragic consequences of an adulterous love affair between Jupiter, the King of the Gods, and Semele, an all too mortal princess. In his introductory argument to the opera, Congreve himself gives a brief outline of the plot of his opera and also details the changes he made to Ovid's account of the myth of Semele:

After Jupiter's Amour with Europa, the Daughter of Agenor, King of Phaenicia, he again incenses Juno by a new Affair in the same Family; *viz.* with Semele, Niece to Europa, and Daughter to Cadmus King of Thebes. Semele is on the Point of Marriage with Athamas; which Marriage is about to be solemniz'd in the Temple of Juno, Goddess of Marriages, when Jupiter by ill Omens interrupts the Ceremony; and afterwards transports Semele to a private Abode prepar'd for her. Juno, after many Contrivances, at length assumes the Shape and Voice of Ino, Sister to Semele; by the help of which Disguise and Artful Insinuations, she prevails with her to make a Request to Jupiter, which being granted must end in her utter Ruin.

This Fable is related in Ovid. Metam. L.3. but there Juno is said to impose on Semele in the Shape of an old Woman, her Nurse. 'Tis hoped, the Liberty taken in substituting Ino instead of the old Woman will be excus'd: It was done, because Ino is interwoven in the Design by her love of Athamas; to whom she was married, according to Ovid; and, because her Character bears a Proportion with the Dignity of the other Persons represented. This Reason, it is presumed, may be allowed in a Thing intirely fictitious; and more especially being represented under the Title of an Opera, where greater Absurdities are every day excused.

[vol. 3, p. 89]

Congreve's summary gives no more than the bare bones of the plot, the simple narrative framework around which he has woven the complex and subtle fabric of his text. For instance, what is significant about the opening scene is not that a marriage is about to be solemnised between Semele and Prince Athamas, but that Semele is being pressed into this marriage against her will by Athamas and by her father, King Cadmus. Her hesitation stems from the fact that she has already been subjected to Jupiter's amorous attentions: Jupiter has whetted Semele's appetite and inflamed her ambition to the extent that she is quite indifferent to the attractive qualities of an eligible young prince. She now feels confused as to what this all-powerful God requires of her. He very soon makes his intentions clear by dousing the sacred flames on Juno's altar with a shower of rain and then destroying Juno's statue with a thunderbolt. Shortly afterwards, he intervenes even more directly, swooping down to earth in the guise of an eagle to carry Semele off to a palace he has built for her on Mount Citheron. Meanwhile, Ino, Semele's sister, confesses to Prince Athamas that she has secretly been in love with him, even while pleading on his behalf to her less than enthusiastic sister.

Act 2 opens with Juno, Jupiter's almost insanely jealous wife, scheming with Iris how to eject Semele, the latest adulteress from her husband's bed. Iris tells her of the extreme measures Jupiter has taken to prevent unwelcome intrusions into his love nest:

> With Adamant the Gates are barr'd,
> Whose Entrance two fierce Dragons guard:
> At each approach they lash their forky Stings,
> And clap their brazen Wings:
> And as their scaly Horrours rise,
> They all at once disclose
> A thousand fiery Eyes,
> Which never know Repose.
>
> [vol. 3, p. 98]

In order to quieten these ferocious dragons, Juno resolves to enlist the help of Somnus, God of Sleep.

The remainder of Act 2, shows us Semele enjoying all the delights of erotic love, including the instant reliving of her latest amorous toils in her dreams. As soon as she wakes from a voluptuous dream, Jupiter is there in the flesh to bring her new delights. Despite such endless pleasure, Semele is not entirely satisfied. She is concerned at her ambiguous position, caught between the human and the godlike, and is keen to bridge the gulf between the two by achieving the full status of immortality. Jupiter views this as a dangerous ambition and at once resolves to distract her with new and varied pleasures. He begins by spiriting her sister, Ino, from below to join them and to provide company and entertainment for Semele. He transports them both to Arcadia where they are diverted by dances and rural sports.

Act 3 begins in Somnus's cave with Juno attempting to rouse Somnus so that she may bribe him into helping her obtain revenge. She offers him the nymph, Pasithea, in return for which he is to relinquish to her his leaden rod, with which Juno will quieten the two dragons guarding Semele's palace; he is also to ensure that Jupiter is roused to a frenzy of desire by erotic dreams and that Ino is kept firmly asleep. Armed with Somnus's agreement, and disguised as Ino, Juno sets off for Semele's palace. Her intention is to fire Semele's desire to become immortal. Significantly, even before Juno's arrival Semele confesses that she is already dying for 'the Joys of Ambition'. Juno therefore has a relatively easy task. She only has to show Semele a flattering image of herself in a mirror to convince her that she is irresistible.

Her cruel scheme for disposing of Semele is to persuade her that Jupiter's divine essence will be passed to her if she can make him come to her bed in all his divine glory. Juno knows full well that Semele's mortal frame cannot withstand the effects of being confronted by Jupiter, the mighty thunderer. She advises Semele to deny Jupiter any further erotic favours until he agrees to grant whatever she asks, and then to make him swear by the Styx that he will carry out his promise. With some venom, Juno adds a pointed reference to herself:

> Conjure him by his Oath
> Not to approach your Bed
> In likeness of a Mortal,
> But like himself, the mighty Thunderer
> In Pomp of Majesty,
> And heav'nly Attire;
> As when he proud *Saturnia* charms,
> And with ineffable Delights
> Fills her encircling Arms,
> And pays the Nuptial Rites.
> [Act 3, Scene 3, vol. 3, p. 106]

Semele eagerly accepts Juno's advice and in so doing sets up her own death. When Jupiter comes to her, sexually roused by Somnus's dreams, he is willing to grant her anything. Too late he realises what she desires, and then attempts to reason with her. He knows only too well the effects that his mighty thunder will have on her. But her ambition makes her blind to reason, and she insists that he carry out his promise. Grief-stricken, Jupiter resolves to try his softest lightning and his mildest melting bolt; but he knows in his heart that 'She must a Victim fall'.

In the closing scenes of the opera, Semele begins to repent of her folly but is duly consumed in flames when Jupiter appears above her. Ino is wafted back to earth and tells Cadmus and Athamas that Hermes has informed her of Semele's fate. He has also told her that Jupiter wishes her to marry Athamas. The final scene shows Apollo announcing the birth of Bacchus from Semele's ashes:

> From Tyrannous Love all your Sorrows proceed,
> From Tyrannous Love you shall quickly be freed.
> From *Semele*'s Ashes a *Phœnix* shall rise,
> The Joy of this earth, and Delight of the skies:
> A God he shall prove
> More mighty than Love,
> And a Sovereign Juice shall invent,
> Which Antidote pure
> The sick Lover shall cure,
> And Sighing and Sorrow for ever prevent.
> Then Mortals be merry, and scorn the Blind Boy;
> Your Hearts from his Arrows strong Wine shall defend:
> Each Day and each Night you shall revel in Joy,
> For when *Bacchus* is born, Love's Reign's at an end.
>
> [vol. 3, p. 110]

The jaunty drinking song with which the opera closes underlines the deliberate artifice of the ending. As in his masque, *The Judgement of Paris*, the original Greek myth has a much darker outcome than the ending of the opera suggests. The myth tells how Juno, not content with Semele's death, is enraged that Jupiter rescues Bacchus, Semele's unborn child, from the flames. (Jupiter kept the foetus in his thigh until the child was fully formed.) After his birth, Bacchus is brought up by Ino and Athamas. Juno's fury at this further betrayal by Jupiter provokes her into persecuting Bacchus throughout his life; she also drives Ino and Athamas into committing suicide for their part in nurturing Bacchus. None of this is suggested in the light-hearted drinking song with which the opera concludes. Congreve deliberately allows a baroque sense of artistic festivity to triumph over chaos and destruction. With its splendid staging effects and resonant dialogue, Congreve's opera was clearly conceived as an aesthetic transcendence of tragedy and death.

However, the darker sides of the story are more clearly spelled out than in *The Judgement of Paris*. When Semele falls a victim to Jupiter's thunderbolt, she is destroyed not only by fire, but even more by her own all too human ambition. Not content to be the wife of a mortal prince, she aspires to be Jupiter's mistress and then even his wife. Not content with enjoying all the sensual delights that Jupiter can offer her, not content with carrying Jupiter's child, she still longs for the unattainable gift of immortality. It is this restless ambition that makes her such an easy prey for Juno.

Juno, for her part, rampages through the opera as a destructive and passionately vengeful force. Despite her divine status, her responses are reminiscent of those of a Lady Touchwood or a Queen Zara. Unlike these two figures, she cannot even presume to harm or hurt her all-powerful husband; but she can use every conceivable strategy to destroy those on whom he has bestowed his favours. She is yet another of Congreve's passionately jealous female figures who casts a baleful shadow over all she touches. Even Jupiter confesses to Semele that it was Juno's excessive jealousy that in the first place drove him out of Elysium.

Despite his undoubted powers, Jupiter or Jove as he is frequently called in the text, emerges as a gentle and considerate lover. Semele represents something very special for him, and he is prepared to do all he can to satisfy her every whim. His unhappy marriage to Juno, to which he nevertheless remains firmly committed, is an obvious reflection of the many aristocratic and royal marriages of Congreve's own period. The function of such marriages was to guarantee social order, hierarchy and stability: personal happiness and fulfilment was not a necessary part of the equation. That would be found, if at all, outside the normal confines of a formal marriage. Jupiter is a typical baroque king who would never allow his marriage to be threatened but whose appetite for sensual pleasure led him to seek for sexual partners who would be flattered by his attentions. Semele is just such a partner; unfortunately, she fails to understand the basic rules of the game. Her aim is to become immortal and to usurp Juno's place. That is something Jupiter will not and cannot tolerate.

The baroque texture of the opera is suggested very clearly in Congreve's unusually detailed stage directions. Full use is made of the scenic stage, its lighting and pyrotechnic effects, as well as of cloud machines and complete scenic transformations. The most spectacular effects are reserved for the end of Act 3. Juno appears ascending in her chariot and gloats over her rival, Semele, who is just about to meet her end. After she ascends, the following directions describe Semele's end:

> *The Scene opening discovers Semele lying under a Canopy, leaning pensively. While a mournful Symphony is playing she looks up and sees Jupiter descending in a black Cloud; the motion of the Cloud is slow. Flashes of lightning issue from either side, and thunder is heard grumbling in the air [. . .] As the Cloud which contains Jupiter is arrived just over the Canopy of Semele, a sudden and great Flash of Lightning breaks forth, and a Clap of loud Thunder is heard; when at one instant Semele with the Palace and whole present Scene disappear, and Jupiter re-ascends swiftly. The Scene totally changed represents a pleasant Country, Mount Citheron closing the Prospect.*
>
> [vol. 3, p. 109]

Finally Apollo's entry is prepared in an equally spectacular manner:

> *A bright Cloud descends and rests on Mount Citheron, which opening, discovers Apollo seated in it as the God of Prophecy.*
>
> [vol. 3, p. 110]

The staging effects make it very clear that Congreve intended his opera to be seen as a festive baroque celebration of art triumphing over the forces of death and destruction.

Within this sumptuous setting, and often hidden beneath the sonorities of the flowery verse, Congreve permitted himself a number of delightfully ironic touches, particularly in the way he handled erotic imagery. For instance, when Semele wakes from her erotic dreams, she is so pleased with the recollection, that she rebukes sleep for leaving her and removing its visionary joys. Equally, when Jupiter comes to her at the end of the opera, he has been so roused by frustrating erotic dreams that he is 'all over Fire' and wishes at once to retire to bed with her. Even Juno manages some oblique erotic references, particularly when dealing with Somnus. At one point, she peremptorily instructs him to resign to her his 'leaden Rod', leaving the audience to savour the obvious double meaning.

The pivotal scene in which Semele and Jupiter revel in their love amounts to a frank and explicit affirmation of sexual delight: even the rhythm of the verse echoes that of love-making:[5]

> If chearful Hopes
> And chilling Fears,
> Alternate Smiles,
> Alternate Tears,
> Eager Panting,
> Fond Desiring,
> With Grief now fainting,
> Now with Bliss expiring;
> If this be Love, not you alone,
> But Love and I are one.
> [Act 2, Scene 3; vol. 3, p. 100]

This was Congreve's final exuberant celebration of the joys of erotic love, set against a sombre background of betrayal, jealousy and death.

In *Semele* Congreve had written a final warning to his contemporaries (and to himself) on the dangers of succumbing to the forces of appetite and ambition. Paradoxically, it was a lack of ambition on the part of the composer, John Eccles, that almost certainly delayed the completion of his setting of Congreve's libretto; it would appear that at this stage of his career, Eccles was more interested in the pastoral pleasures of fishing on the Thames at Kingston than in composing.[6] As a result, Congreve's contemporaries were denied the privilege of savouring the delights of *Semele* in production.[7]

It fell to Handel to give renewed life to Congreve's libretto in 1744 (albeit in a version probably altered by his librettist Newburgh Hamilton to suit the more puritan tastes of the mid-eighteenth century). It is this setting of *Semele* that has found an increasingly enthusiastic response from both performers and audiences in the latter part of the twentieth century. Congreve's sonorous verse and deliberate use of a festive baroque setting for his opera, (beautifully mirrored in Handel's flawlessly stylish setting), seem to express an almost Nietzschean sense of art transcending the absurdity of death and destruction; such a view of art has clearly found its proper resonance in the sensibilities of twentieth-century performers and audiences.

It was entirely fitting that the Royal Opera House, Covent Garden, should choose to celebrate in 1982 the 250th anniversary of the founding of the Covent Garden Theatre (a theatre that had opened in 1732 with a production of *The Way of the World*) with a lavish production of the Congreve/Handel version of *Semele*. In terms of singing, acting and staging, this gala production did full justice to the splendid baroque theatricality of Congreve's libretto. Some 280 years after the opera was completed, *Semele* was at last given the kind of production on the London stage that Congreve had clearly envisaged when he had prepared his libretto for the opening of London's first opera house in 1705. This production, along with a television documentary account of both opera and production prepared by London Weekend for its South Bank Show, was a moving tribute to a playwright who passionately wished to see a specifically English form of opera developed (in opposition to the dominant Italian mode of *opera seria*) and who was the first to write a full-length opera in English for the London stage.

8
Congreve in Production

The varied fortunes of Congreve's plays at their first performances have already been alluded to in earlier chapters. The comedies, *The Old Batchelour* and *Love for Love*, were immediate and outstanding successes, as was Congreve's tragedy, *The Mourning Bride*. In contrast, the response to the comedies, *The Double Dealer* and *The Way of the World*, was appreciably less warm. These initial responses on the part of London's audiences seem to have established a firm ranking order for the popularity of Congreve's plays that remained virtually unchanged during the first half of the eighteenth century. Up until the 1740s, both *The Old Batchelour* and *Love for Love* were given three times the number of performances of Congreve's remaining three plays.[1] However, after successful revivals of *The Way of the World* and *The Double Dealer* in 1718 and of *The Mourning Bride* in 1719, all of Congreve's plays featured on a regular basis in the repertoire of London's theatres until the 1760s.

In his seminal study of Congreve's plays on the eighteenth-century stage, Emmett Avery has calculated that in 1714 Congreve's five plays made up 4 per cent of total performances in London; by 1720 this had risen to 5.1 per cent; by the late 1730s the proportion was as high as 6.1 per cent. Thereafter a gradual decline set in until the concluding years of the eighteenth century when his plays were performed only infrequently.[2] What these figures demonstrate is the continued theatrical appeal of Congreve's plays long after the social and political presuppositions that underpinned his work had disappeared. Even changes in audience taste and sensibility, in particular the growing preference for sentimental and improving drama in the early decades of the eighteenth century, do not appear to have substantially affected the popularity of his plays until the 1760s. And it was not until the 1770s that bowdlerised and altered versions of his plays were prepared for performance in London.

Throughout the eighteenth century, the appeal of Congreve's plays lay in the splendid acting roles they afforded contemporary players, and notably the leading actresses of each generation. Once specific roles were assigned to individual actors in the theatres of Restoration and Georgian London, these normally became their property in that particular theatre until such time as they chose to relinquish them. Inevitably, there were some changes in cast lists every season, as actors retired or switched their allegiance to the rival London playhouse. But, in the main, one of the attractions for London audiences in attending revivals of well-known plays was the opportunity to experience once again the interpretation offered by a popular acting star or a familiar group of actors. (That same pleasure sustains today's video and recording industry.)

Additional excitement was generated on those occasions when the two patent theatres in London decided to mount rival productions of the same play, or when a key actor relinquished an important part to a rival, and normally younger, player. The latter was the case with *Love for Love* in February 1708 at Drury Lane when London audiences flocked to see Anne Oldfield take over the role of Angelica which had previously belonged exclusively to Anne Bracegirdle for whom the part was written.

There was no love lost between these two actresses. Contemporary accounts suggest that Anne Oldfield was an ambitious and ruthless young lady who was quite prepared to elbow her way forward: there is even some evidence to indicate that her relentless jockeying for position in Owen Swiney's company at the Queen's Theatre may have contributed to Anne Bracegirdle's sudden decision to retire from the stage in 1707.[3] In view of the gossip surrounding Anne Bracegirdle's retirement, London audiences were understandably curious to see what Anne Old-field made of the role of Angelica: it would seem from her continuing popularity in this role that she did not disappoint them.

By the time she played Millamant in the 1718 revival of *The Way of the World*, Anne Oldfield had established a firm reputation for herself as one of the leading actresses on the London stage. The attraction for London audiences on this occasion was to see what she would make of Millamant in her own right and especially when partnered by the elegant and popular John Wilks as Mirabell. Their performance was sufficiently well-received to ensure that *The Way of the World* was revived in every season during the 1720s.

John Rich's decision to open his new playhouse, the Theatre Royal, Covent Garden, in 1732 with a production of *The Way of the World* helped to secure the continuing popularity of the work throughout the 1730s. During the same decade there were also regular performances of Congreve's remaining plays, including a new production of *The Double Dealer* at Drury Lane in 1735,[4] and a performance of *The Mourning Bride*, with royalty present, on 24 February 1737, in honour of Mrs Porter.[5]

By the time Garrick assumed, with James Lacy, the position of joint manager of the Theatre Royal, Drury Lane in 1747, the popularity of Congreve's plays had begun to wane. Garrick himself showed little interest in Congreve's comedies, taking on only small character roles. However in the 1750–1 season he organised revivals of both *The Way of the World* and *The Mourning Bride*. One of his leading actresses, Mrs Pritchard played Millamant in *The Way of the World* and Zara in *The Mourning Bride*, while Garrick himself decided to play the role of Osmyn in *The Mourning Bride*. Francis Gentleman in *The Dramatic Censor* had mixed feelings about both Mrs Pritchard's and Garrick's performances in Congreve's tragedy. Describing Mrs Pritchard's performance, he stated:

> Mrs PRITCHARD was majestic, but rather too corpulent; in speaking and acting the part, she shewed correct and fine preservation of character. The amorous passages were indeed not so harmonious as might be wished, but in the jealousy she made ample amends.[6]

In respect of Garrick, he commented:

> Mr GARRICK, we think, in the soliloquies, and the scene with Heli, outstripped every competitor; but the Moorish habit proved rather too much for his figure, and the amorous passages did not flow from him with that natural sincerity, of which Mr BARRY gave us an ample and very pleasing idea.[7]

Miss Bellamy who was cast as Almeria was considered a weak choice by the actor-manager Tate Wilkinson who saw the production in 1750, 'Miss Bellamy very inferior indeed to Mrs Cibber'.[8] However, despite such reservations the production ran for thirteen performances during the season and attracted good box-office receipts.[9] [See Plate 1.]

The 1760s and 1770s saw a further decline in the popularity of Congreve's plays, although there were still occasional revivals that attracted audience interest and critical attention. At times such revivals were used to give prominence to the work of a leading actress. Such was, for instance, the case with Mrs Abington, a gifted but mercurial actress, who caused endless trouble and vexation to Garrick but who enjoyed a devoted following, particularly amongst the ladies, to whom she seemed, despite her lowly origins, a perfect model of fashion and good taste.

Interestingly, the Congreve roles she enjoyed best were not only Millamant in *The Way of the World* but also Miss Prue in *Love for Love*. In the latter part she was able to outshine any rival actress playing the role of Angelica, as she first discovered in Dublin in 1769.[10] Presumably she indulged in a similar process of upstaging when she acted the same part at Drury Lane in November 1769 and November 1776. [See Plate 2.] One of her contemporary admirers, Thomas Davies, was struck by her versatility in taking on this role:

> From an actress celebrated for characters of high life, and eminent for graceful deportment and elegant action, you would not expect the awkward and petulant behaviour of a girl just come from a farmhouse: Mrs Abington, unconfined in her talents, rendered Miss Prue as naturally rude and diverting, as if she had been mistress of no other style in acting than rustic simplicity.[11]

Plate 1   Garrick as Osmyn and Miss Bellamy as Almeria in *The Mourning Bride.*

Plate 2   Mrs Abington as Miss Prue in *Love for Love*.

Plate 3 Mrs Pitt as Lady Wishfort and Mrs Green as Foible in *The Way of the World*.

Plate 4   Samuel Foote as Fondlewife, James Aickin as Bellmour and Mrs Gardner as Laetitia in *The Old Batchelour.*

A month later, at the end of December 1776, when she acted the part of Millamant, she was acclaimed in a published impromptu as the woman who best united in her person both beauty and fashion.[12] Once again Thomas Davies wrote enthusiastically of her performance:

> Congreve's Millamant of past times she has skilfully modelled and adapted to the admired coquette and lovely tyrant of the present day. All ages have their particular colours and variations of follies and fashions; these she understands perfectly, and dresses them to the taste of the present hour.[13]

This production of *The Way of the World* at Drury Lane was a calculated and successful challenge to the Theatre Royal, Covent Garden, which had mounted its version of the play some seven weeks earlier on 2 November 1776. The reviews had been mixed. *The Chronicle* felt that Mrs Barry as Millamant was adequate but unexciting, whereas, 'Mrs Pitt *bawled* out Lady Wishfor't with more applause than she deserved'.[14] [See Plate 3.]

A further series of Congreve revivals was organised in the late 1760s and 1770s by the actor-manager, Samuel Foote. Foote was an enterprising comic actor who had first taken on a number of Congreve's character parts in the 1750s. His managerial ambitions were rewarded in 1766 with a royal patent giving him authority to mount productions of plays at the Little Theatre in the Haymarket during the summer months.[15] His repertoire included revivals of two of Congreve's comedies in which he himself played important character roles: Fondlewife in *The Old Batchelour* between 1769 and 1775 [see Plate 4]; and Sir Paul Plyant in *The Double Dealer* in September 1776. Although he had some success with these productions, his arrogance and satiric disposition had made sufficient enemies for him in the world of the theatre to ensure that his work often met with a less than generous response. In particular, the actor and publisher, Thomas Davies, who was a passionate admirer of Garrick, considered Foote beyond contempt for his disparaging treatment of Garrick. Accordingly he wrote scathingly of Foote's abilities as an actor and, in particular, took a dim view of his approach to Congreve's character roles:

Sometimes he ventured on some important parts in old comedies, such as Fondlewife in the Old Bachelor, Sir Paul Pliant in the Double Dealer, and Ben in Love for Love. His intimacy with people of the first rank contributed to support him in his feeble attempts upon the masterly characters of Congreve; and it will scarce be credited, that for three nights the boxes were crowded, to see Foote murder the part of Ben; for his acting bore no resemblance to nature and character. He was even destitute of what no man could suppose him to want, a proper confidence in his own abilities; for sure his Ben was as unentertaining a lump of insipidity as ever a patient audience was presented with; it was not even a lively mistake of humour.

In his Fondlewife he had luckily remembered that great master of acting, Colley Cibber. In the course of the first scene, he drew the attention of the audience, and merited, and gained much applause; but, in the progress of the part, he forgot his exemplar, and degenerated into buffoonery. His Sir Paul Pliant was worse, if possible, than his Ben; for fear restrained him from being outrageous in the sailor: but in the Knight he gave a loose to the most ridiculous burlesque and vilest grimace. However, the people laughed heartily, and that, he thought, was a full approbation of his grotesque performance. In short, Foote was a despicable player in almost all parts but those which he wrote for himself.[16]

From the 1780s both Sarah Siddons and her brother, John Philip Kemble, breathed new life, albeit infrequently, into Congreve's work. In the case of Mrs Siddons, she made a triumphant return to the London stage in 1782–3 after her initial disastrous London début and several years spent touring the provinces. For her second benefit performance at Drury Lane that season she chose to act the part of Zara in *The Mourning Bride* in March 1783 and received 'expressions of admiration from persons of rank and talent'.[17] Her success in this part provoked the management of Covent Garden Theatre in 1784 to mount a rival production of *The Mourning Bride* and to import Mrs Crawford from Ireland to play Almeria for a single performance of the play on 5 February.

Kemble, who made his London début in the role of Hamlet in 1783, was to become, like his sister, best known as a tragic actor.

However, in 1787, he took the role of Valentine in a production of *Love for Love* at Drury Lane and, in a review published in the *World*, received warm praise for his acting:

> In the *acting*, there is abundant merit. The Valentine of *Kemble*, is perfect in all its parts. The ease, the elegance, the strong sense, and feeling of the character came up, as Congreve would let them.[18]

In 1789 he took the role of Osmyn for the first time, playing opposite his sister in the role of Zara, in a production of *The Mourning Bride* at Drury Lane that was enthusiastically received.

Kemble retained his interest in Congreve and prepared a revised version of *The Way of the World* for a production at Drury Lane as late as 1800. In 1807 he also once again played the role of Osmyn in a production of *The Mourning Bride* which featured his sister as Zara. A review in the *Monthly Mirror* described them as follows:

> The *Zara* of Mrs Siddons was excellent throughout, but in the scene with *Osmyn*, in the prison, she was wonderfully fine. Mr Kemble wore his Moorish dress with all its advantage, and played with great ability; but in tragedy Mrs Siddons's star has so much the ascendant, as to eclipse every other within the sphere of its lustrous action.[19]

The retirement of Mrs Siddons from the stage in 1812, followed by that of her brother, Kemble, in 1816, marked the final disappearance from the repertoire of *The Mourning Bride*.

In the early part of the nineteenth century, only *Love for Love* and *The Way of the World* were given sporadic performances on the London stage and even then in versions that had been severely cut and rewritten. In the latter part of the nineteenth century, Congreve's plays disappeared altogether from the repertoire of London's theatres. Clearly his frank and satiric dissection of interaction between the sexes was no more acceptable to the delicate sensibilities of Victorian audiences than was to prove the case with Ibsen's equally frank exploration of sexual politics in plays like *A Doll's House* and *Ghosts*.

In the early years of the twentieth century, a number of Congreve revivals were mounted by stage societies. The first was a production of *The Way of the World* by the Mermaid Society in April 1904. Over ten years later, the Stage Society and the Phoenix Society presented a cycle of Congreve productions beginning with *The Double Dealer* in May 1916 and concluding with *The Mourning Bride* in November 1925. All these productions, mainly inspired by the scholarly enthusiasm of Montague Summers, were for club members only. It was not until 1924 that Nigel Playfair's production of *The Way of the World* at the Lyric Theatre, Hammersmith, with Edith Evans as Millamant, re-established Congreve as an author to be reckoned with on the London stage.

Playfair had already mounted a successful revival of *The Beggar's Opera* in the previous season and was confident, despite the scepticism of his financial backers, that he could achieve a similar success with Congreve's play. By his own admission, he 'burlesqued the plot considerably, and treated it as a joke',[20] in order to make it more accessible to a modern audience. At the same time, he recognised in Millamant a character of genuine subtlety, complexity and poignancy. Edith Evans conveyed that subtlety with all the formidable acting skills at her disposal. James Agate in *The Sunday Times* (10 February 1924) wrote enthusiastically of her performance:

Her Millamant is impertinent without being pert, graceless without being ill-graced. She has only two scenes, but what scenes they are of unending subtlety and finesse! Never can that astonishing 'Ah! idle creature, get up when you will' have taken on greater delicacy, nor 'I may by degrees *dwindle* into a wife' a more delicious mockery. '*Adieu*, my morning thoughts, agreeable wakings, indolent slumbers, all ye *douceurs*, ye *sommeils du matin, adieu*' – all this is breathed out as though it were early Ronsard or du Bellay. And 'I nauseate walking', and 'Natural, easy Suckling!' bespeak the very genius of humour. There is a pout of the lips, a jutting forward of the chin to greet the conceit, and a smile of happy deliverance when it is uttered, which defy the chronicler. This face, at such moments, is like a city in illumination, and when it is withdrawn leaves a glow behind.[21]

Playfair's production was revived in 1927, with some changes to the cast, but as in 1924 it was Edith Evans as Millamant who captured the attention of the critics. Looking back on her achievement from the vantage point of the early 1960s, John Gielgud commented:

> Edith Evans's performance as Millamant was probably the finest stylized piece of bravura acting seen in London in the last fifty years. Her economy and grace of movement, her perfectly sustained poses, the purring coquetry of her voice with its extraordinary subtlety of range, was inimitably captivating.[22]

In 1934 Tyrone Guthrie directed an outstanding production of *Love for Love* at the Old Vic, with a distinguished cast that included Flora Robson as Mrs Foresight and Charles Laughton as Tattle. Once again, London's critics were obliged to recognise the brilliance of Congreve's acting roles. Laughton's Tattle, for instance, was described in *The Sunday Times* as:

> a delicious figure of fun and under-breeding, a mixture of wiggery and waggery, at once coy and servile, male yet mincing.[23]

The review in *The Daily Telegraph* acknowledged that there was:

> a delightful sense of style about the whole production, which fits admirably with the brilliance of the author's English and the sureness of his characterisation.[24]

A similar sense of style informed John Gielgud's memorable 1943 revival of *Love for Love* in London. He not only directed the production but also played the role of Valentine, ably assisted by Leon Quartermain as Scandal, Miles Malleson as Foresight and Yvonne Arnaud as Mrs Frail. Looking back on this production in his book, *Stage Directions*, written in 1963, Gielgud commented on the approach he had taken:

> I discussed with Leon Quartermain, who was to play Scandal, how best to set about the direction of it. We both felt that if the actors would all play realistically – and were also stylish enough

to wear their clothes and deport themselves with elegance – there was no reason why we might not play the play in a naturalistic style, with the 'fourth wall down' as it were. This was in direct opposition to anything I had ever seen, for, in Playfair's productions, the asides were delivered (as no doubt they were in the eighteenth century) directly to the audience, and there was no attempt at localization in the settings, which were merely drop scenes and wings, and served as a background (but not as a home) for the characters in the play.[25]

The same desire to find a more naturalistic means of staging Congreve informed Peter Wood's 1965 production of *Love for Love* at the National Theatre. This underlined the social subtext of the piece which Wood saw as a biting satire directed against the materialism of the upper classes in Congreve's day. The setting, costumes, wigs and props were given a battered, worn look; the pace was slowed down to allow room for thought as well as laughter. The critics were divided in their response. Most favoured the attempt to achieve a greater degree of realism while some regretted the loss of comic pace. The production enjoyed a strong cast and, in particular, benefited from the contribution of Laurence Olivier as Tattle. J.C. Trewin in *The Illustrated London News* described him as:

an agile, scandalous cat, now thrusting out a paw, now exploring the roof, now purring secretively, now (as if his tail had been trodden on) wailing in inarticulate despair.[26]

Peter Wood's 1985 revival of his *Love for Love* production at the National Theatre was a distinctly prettified reworking of his original concept. The acting was competent (the cast included Stephen Moore as Valentine, Tim Curry as Tattle and Amanda Redman as Angelica) but, without the extraordinary energy of Laurence Olivier, the actors seemed generally dwarfed by the huge and lavishly detailed set.

Post-war revivals of *The Way of the World*, including John Gielgud's 1953 production of the play for the Lyric, Hammersmith, were initially overshadowed by the legendary achievement of Edith Evans in Nigel Playfair's 1924 production. Arguably it was not until the Royal Shakespeare Company presented John Barton's production at the Aldwych Theatre in 1978 that London audiences were offered significantly new insights into the play. Irving Wardle, in a perceptive review for *The Times* (30 January 1978), outlined what these were:

The most conspicuous novelty among the performances is Michael Pennington's Mirabell. Gielgud has succeeded, and others have tried with less success, to pass off this character as Millamant's equally dazzling partner. But where Millamant lives through her lines, Mirabell lives mainly through the words of others; and Mr Pennington never competes with her. Instead he relaxes into a cool acceptance of his own power, and concentrates on the lover rather than the intriguer. He knows he will win in the end, and waits quietly at the centre of the whirling dance of fools and fops until the delicious bird enters his net. The unnerving thing about Mr Pennington's performance is its apparent sincerity.

The marriage scene remains the jewel of the production, and the high point of Judi Dench's wonderful Millamant, a piece of high-precision sexual engineering constructed from languishing cries, bubbling laughs, instantaneous mood transitions, always in motion with a train like a matador's cloak, designed at once to exert invincible attraction and evade capture. One master-stroke among many is her final compliance with Mirabell: 'I hate your odious provisos.' Even Edith Evans delivered this skittishly: Miss Dench lingers caressingly over it.

As her grotesque erotic counterpart, Beryl Reid achieves extraordinary variety as Lady Wishfort without the usual coarsening of the character. There is a certain level of decorum beneath which Congreve's old harridan does not sink, whether taking her fan to the drunken Sir Wilfull (treated for once with real respect by Bob Peck), or belabouring the treacherous Foible (Eliza Ward) with a hefty stick. The pathos is there as well as the absurdity: expressed in the precipitous slips of her genteel vowels. The performance is full of robust invention: 'Nothing so alluring as a *levée* from a couch', she declares, vainly struggling to get up.[27]

This splendid achievement was matched by a 1975 Thames Television production of *The Way of the World*, directed by

Peter Duguid, with Alan Howard as Mirabell, Gemma Jones as Millamant, John Moffatt as Witwoud and Irene Worth as Lady Wishfort. The naturalistic medium of television was used to good effect to recreate, with loving attention to detail, the interior of Lady Wishfort's town house, while the Mall scenes were shot in the formal gardens of Hidcote Manor, near Stratford. The acting was informed by an equally meticulous attention to detail, and was based on a clear understanding of the complex way in which the various characters interact. In addition, some particularly fine camera work helped to clarify the emotional subtext at moments of particular significance; for instance, highlighting the mixed emotions experienced by Mrs Fainall when Millamant finally agrees to marry Mirabell. This production demonstrated that the intimate quality of Congreve's writing in *The Way of the World* was well suited to the intimate nature of television as a medium.

Congreve's remaining two comedies, *The Old Batchelour* and *The Double Dealer* have been less frequently revived. Surprisingly, *The Old Batchelour*, which was Congreve's most popular play in the early part of the eighteenth century, has enjoyed only one professional revival this century. Nigel Playfair mounted a production of the play at the Lyric, Hammersmith, in 1931 (with a cut and revised text) in which some of the minor roles were played by the most distinguished actors: Miles Malleson as Sir Joseph Wittol; O. B. Clarence as Fondlewife and Edith Evans as Laetitia. Given the outstanding quality of such actors in these character roles, it is hardly surprising that the production was widely acclaimed.[28]

It was not until August 1959 that *The Double Dealer* was given its first major London revival at the Old Vic. Michael Benthall directed an impressive cast with due regard to what one critic called the play's 'crazy joy in life'.[29] Donald Houston played Maskwell; Ursula Jeans, Lady Touchwood; and once again Miles Malleson played yet another Congreve character role, this time Sir Paul Plyant, with his usual brilliance. A second London production of the play followed ten years later in 1969 at the National Theatre and included Judy Parfitt as Lady Touchwood and John Castle as Maskwell.

The most recent production of *The Double Dealer*, a touring production originating from the Wolsey Theatre, Ipswich, in 1991, stressed the raw physical energy in the play. Nichola

McAuliffe as Lady Touchwood and Steven Mann as Maskwell gave a flamboyantly erotic account of their dangerous and predatory relationship, while Paul Eddington gave a poignantly bumbling interpretation of Sir Paul Plyant. The production was directed by his daughter, Gemma Eddington, with considerable inventiveness and vigour. Its only weakness lay in the portrayal of the central characters Mellefont and Cynthia (respectively Michael Hobbs and Kate Godfrey) who seemed excessively pale and drab in the shadow of these more energetically portrayed figures.

While Congreve's comedies were given sparkling revivals on the London stage from the mid-1920s onwards, it has taken far longer to achieve revivals of similar stature for his opera and masque libretti. This is in large measure due to the fact that London audiences have only in the past few decades begun to show a growing enthusiasm for English baroque music. Previously this was a minority interest, largely confined to university music societies. Hence it comes as no surprise to discover that the first stage performance of *Semele* was given by the Cambridge University Musical Society in 1925. Even the first major London production of *Semele* in 1959 was given at Sadler's Wells Theatre by a group of Handel specialists, the Handel Opera Society under Charles Farncombe, to mark the bicentenary of Handel's death. It was not until 1970 that Sadler's Wells Opera mounted a production of *Semele* as part of their normal repertoire at the Coliseum: Charles Mackerras was the conductor and Filippo Sanjust the director. Finally, in 1982 the Royal Opera House, Covent Garden, mounted a lavish production of *Semele* to commemorate the 250th anniversary of the founding of Covent Garden Theatre.

Charles Mackerras was once again the conductor and paid meticulous attention on this occasion to the ornate baroque qualities of Handel's music, in particular to the way the arias lend themselves, in the *da capo* repeats, to baroque embellishment on the part of the soloists. The designer, Henry Bardon, based his set designs, despite the difference in size and scale, on stage-settings from the eighteenth-century court theatre at Drottningholm near Stockholm. The effect was visually enchanting as a series of baroque exterior settings, complete with a cloud machine for the Goddess Iris, were contrasted with Semele's sumptuous bedroom. The costumes designed by David Walker were flamboyantly baroque in conception and greatly assisted the singers' approach to characterisation. The director, John Copley, concentrated on bringing out the all too human implications of Semele's affair with Jupiter, giving due weight to their mutually shared erotic delight but also stressing Semele's fatal ambition. Jupiter was sung by the tenor, Robert Tear, Semele by the soprano, Valerie Masterson, and Juno by the American mezzo, Kathleen Kuhlmann. Their performances were sparkling, both in terms of their singing and in terms of the emotional subtlety they communicated in their acting. A South Bank Show programme, screened on 9 January 1983 (directed by Tony Cash for London Weekend), provided a documentary record of the meticulous preparatory work that went into this production, while also conveying something of the flavour of the stage performance.

The 1989 promenade concert season at the Royal Albert Hall brought an equally festive revival of Congreve's masque *The Judgement of Paris*. On Sunday, 13 August 1989, a group of singers and players recreated a semi-staged version of the musical competition first held in London in 1701. Three musical settings of Congreve's text were played in sequence; the composers being Daniel Purcell, John Weldon and John Eccles. A simple staircase set was constructed on the podium of the Albert Hall, which permitted the singers to move freely and adopt a variety of formal blocking patterns. A sense of location and period was conveyed by the baroque costumes worn by the singers. Lorna Marshall was the movement consultant; and Anthony Rooley directed the Consort of Musicke and the Concerto Köln. In each of the three versions, Venus was sung by Emma Kirkby, Pallas by Evelyn Tubb and Juno by Sarah Pendlebury: in contrast, the parts of Mercury and Paris were taken by different male singers for each version. Subtle changes in movement and blocking for each of the three versions added to the differences. Writing in *The Independent* on 12 August, 1989, Anthony Rooley drew attention to the experimental nature of the undertaking:

> Will modern opinion concur with the taste of 1701? This is an experiment, the nearest an artistic project can come to a scientifically controlled set of circumstances. The libretto is constant (a brilliant piece of work by the virtuoso wordsmith,

Congreve), the singers for the three Goddesses remain the same
[. . .], the orchestration has only small variations. So we, the
modern jury – that is, the Prom audience – can listen to three
works written concurrently, reflecting the corporate stylistic
awareness of the age and reflecting three very different
individuals. What better chance could we have to tune into a
lost generation?

While there is no record of the mechanism used to record the
votes of the 1701 audience, the issue was decided in 1989 by the
simple expedient of measuring the decibel level of applause given
to each piece. In the event, there was no difference in the
measured level of applause for the Weldon and the Eccles
versions, which left the presenter with the task of deciding the
issue. In 1701 the competition was won by Weldon, although
many contemporaries preferred the Eccles version; in 1989, on
the decision of the presenter, the competition was indeed won,
albeit narrowly, by the John Eccles version. What this experiment
was able to demonstrate is that the musical taste of a London
audience in 1989 was not significantly different from that of a
London audience in 1701.

The same lesson may, with advantage, be applied to modern
productions of Congreve's plays. It is often wrongly assumed that
the taste of London's discerning theatre-goers in 1700 was
fundamentally different from that of discerning theatre-goers
today. It is also wrongly assumed, in particular by some actors
and directors, that the acting style of the 1690s was fundamentally
different from a modern acting style. Both assumptions are
misplaced. It is very clear from contemporary descriptions of
the leading actors of the 1690s, namely Thomas Betterton and
Elizabeth Barry, that what they aimed for in their acting, and what
their contemporaries valued in their work, was emotional integrity
and intensity. They prepared their parts with very great care, and
prided themselves on their ability to identify emotionally with the
roles they played. At the same time, they were able to keep their
emotional commitment to their roles firmly within their technical
control. It was that balance that ensured their commanding
presence on stage.[30] Precisely the same balance is required from
a modern actor.

Initially, directors such as Nigel Playfair who first revived Congreve's plays on the London stage were inclined to prettify his work and treat it as if it were a gorgeous chocolate box to be gift-wrapped with bows and frills and ribbons; meanwhile, the individual acting roles were treated as separate cameos to be savoured in isolation. In some more recent productions, actors and directors have moved away from an overtly pretty style, creating instead settings that rely for their effect on simple visual suggestion, and concentrating their main efforts on conveying the emotional truth and complexity of the dialogue.

Too much stress on technique, on rhetoric or period 'style' can detract from the emotional truth that lies at the heart of Congreve's plays. The task confronting actors and directors in presenting a Congreve play is the same today as it was in the 1690s. The intricate details of the plot need to be communicated swiftly and directly; a firm physical and visual framework for each character needs to be established and elaborated; above all, however, the complex emotional and social issues that are addressed and explored in each of the plays need to be communicated to an audience with a carefully judged combination of subtlety and committed energy. That is the challenge posed by Congreve in production, and it is one to which a number of modern actors and directors have begun to respond with flair and imagination.

9
Critical Responses

Congreve wrote his plays just before the twin disciplines of literary and theatrical criticism were properly established. Throughout the seventeenth century, literary criticism was primarily viewed as a prescriptive activity, concerned with determining the basic norms and rules of a neoclassic approach to writing. The function of a literary critic was therefore to lay down guidelines and precepts for writers rather than to interpret and explain the work of writers to a reading public. This was as true of an English neoclassicist such as Ben Jonson at the beginning of the century as it was of a French neoclassicist such as Boileau at the end. Even Congreve's own essay, *Concerning Humour in Comedy*, belongs within this prescriptive tradition.

Critical responses to new works tended to be expressed in poems or epigrams rather than in pieces of descriptive analysis. Hence one finds the initial response to Congreve's plays, on the part of his contemporaries, in a series of commendatory verses addressed to the poet. By and large these were fulsome and effusive in their praise of the young author. What impressed Congreve's contemporaries (as it was later to impress Samuel Johnson) is that he achieved his dramatic mastery by his early twenties. Even John Dryden, the elderly Tory and Jacobite doyen amongst the men of letters, was swift to recognise in the young Whig, Congreve, an undisputed and worthy successor to himself as the leading poet of his age. In a poem he addressed to

Congreve for publication with the text of *The Double Dealer*,
he was unstinting in his accolade:

> Firm *Dorique* Pillars found Your solid Base:
> The Fair *Corinthian* Crowns the higher Space;
> Thus all below is Strength, and all above is Grace.
> In easie Dialogue is *Fletcher's* Praise:
> He mov'd the mind, but had not power to raise.
> Great *Johnson* did by strength of Judgment please:
> Yet doubling *Fletcher's* Force, he wants his Ease.
> In differing Tallents both adorn'd their Age;
> One for the Study, t'other for the Stage.
> But both to *Congreve* justly shall submit,
> One match'd in Judgment, both o'er-match'd in Wit.
> In Him all Beauties of this Age we see;
> *Etherege* his Courtship, *Southern's* Purity;
> The Satire, Wit, and Strength of Manly *Witcherly*.
> All this in blooming Youth you have Atchiev'd;
> Now are your foil'd Contemporaries griev'd;
> So much the sweetness of your manners move,
> We cannot envy you because we Love.[1]

Dryden was not alone in penning such verses. Other writers,
including Southerne and Swift, wrote with no less enthusiasm of
their warm response to Congreve's work.

It was not until the Jeremy Collier controversy in 1698 that any
serious objections to Congreve's plays were expressed in writing.
Collier's treatise *The Immorality and Profaneness of the English
Stage* combined a strong sense of political and moral outrage.
Conceived as a secular sermon rather than as a piece of literary
criticism, it nevertheless exploited the techniques of primitive
critical deconstruction, first pioneered by the scholar, Thomas
Rymer, in the 1670s.

Rymer's aim in his tracts, *The Tragedies of the Last Age
consider'd and examin'd by the Practice of the Ancients and by
the Common Sense of all Ages* (1678) and *A Short View of
Tragedy* (1693), was to discredit the creative achievements of the
Moderns by measuring them against the strict neoclassic rules of
the Ancients. Armed with the unities of Time, Place and Action
and the subsidiary demands of order, symmetry, decorum, ideal

truth, and poetic justice, Rymer swept aside even the greatest achievements of Shakespeare and his contemporaries with a rare and quite breathtaking combination of literal-minded pedantry and reformist zeal.

This was essentially the methodology that Collier took over; all he needed for his purposes was to add a battery of puritan moral injunctions to the formidable armoury of neoclassicist rules, and he was able to outdo even Rymer's pedantry and zeal in his desire to convey the works of modern playwrights to the dustbin of history. Congreve's work, along with that of his most distinguished contemporaries, was measured against Collier's absolute moral standards and was found to be woefully deficient. Quoting lines out of context, looking everywhere for examples of blasphemy and smut, Collier had a field-day. Not averse to sarcasm and even downright knockabout, he laid into Congreve and his Whig friends with obvious and genuine relish. There is no appreciation of dramatic subtlety in his work, no understanding of a contextually based justification for satire and laughter. His is essentially the kindergarten approach to literary criticism of the blinkered moralist who has a firm and inflexible scale of values against which to measure all literary creations and, at the same time, a distinctly unhealthy and even prurient fascination for the forbidden fruit he so roundly condemns.[2]

Thanks largely to his robust polemic style, Collier established a long-lasting tradition of simplistic judgemental response that was to disfigure so much of English literary criticism throughout the Georgian and Victorian periods. Echoes of his view of Congreve, in particular, can be traced during the whole of the eighteenth century and well into the Victorian period.

Thomas Macaulay, for instance, writing for *The Edinburgh Review* in 1841, was no less severe than Collier in his critique of Congreve. At least he had the good grace to acknowledge Collier as his critical mentor:

> There is hardly any book of that time from which it would be possible to select specimens of writing so excellent and so various. To compare Collier with Pascal would indeed be absurd. Yet we hardly know where, except in the *Provincial Letters*, we can find mirth so harmoniously and becomingly blended with solemnity as in the *Short View*. [. . .] He

[Congreve] was precisely in that situation in which it is madness to attempt a vindication; for his guilt was so clear, that no address or eloquence could obtain an acquittal.[3]

Viewed from the perspective of Utopian moral absolutes, Congreve was seen as irredeemably guilty; a harmful corrupter of young minds; a man whose plays were an affront to decency and all the more dangerous for being superficially witty and attractive.

As an ironic footnote to this sorry history of self-righteous cant, masquerading as critical commentary, one finds, in the very year before Collier published his attack, an amateur defender of virtue praising Congreve's tragedy, *The Mourning Bride*, for its moral propriety and exemplary qualities. Sir Richard Blackmore, in his preface to *King Arthur* of 1697, commented:

This *Poem* has receiv'd, and in my Opinion very justly, Universal Applause [. . .] The *Diction* is Proper, Clear, Beautiful, Noble, and diversify'd agreeably to the variety of the Subject. Vice, as it ought to be, is punish'd, and Opprest Innocence at last Rewarded. Nature appears very happily imitated, excepting one or two doubtful Instances, thro' the whole Piece, in all which there are no immodest Images or Expressions, no wild, unnatural Rants, but some few Exceptions being allow'd, all things are Chast, Just, and Decent. [. . .] And now there is some reason to hope that our *Poets* will follow this excellent Example, and that hereafter no slovenly Writer will be so hardy as to offer to our Publick Audiences his obscene and prophane Pollutions, to the great Offence of all Persons of Vertue and good Sense.[4]

Needless to say, this more generous, if equally naive, view of Congreve's play was not shared by Collier and his supporting band of moral zealots.

As already described in Chapter 5, Collier's baleful influence extended beyond purely literary criticism into the nascent discipline of theatre criticism. His simplistic critical methodology and his belief in equally simplistic moral absolutes underpin much of the early work undertaken by writers such as Steele and Addison in *The Spectator* and *The Tatler*: they also resurface in

Aaron Hill's journal, *The Prompter*, in the 1730s. However, by
the 1750s a generation of writers emerges who may properly be
called England's first professional theatre critics. Amongst these,
there are some who demonstrate a refreshingly sound critical
judgement in their reviews, and who take seriously the task of
analysing and elucidating to their readers the complexities and
subtleties of the plays performed in London's theatres. Foremost
was Arthur Murphy, who, having failed at a number of careers,
wrote a series of splendid reviews in the late 1750s for Dodsley's
London Chronicle. In these Murphy not only gave a detailed
descriptive account of the contribution made by the actors in a
given production, but he also attempted to wrestle with the work
of the playwright.

In his review of *Love for Love* played at Covent Garden
Theatre in October 1758, he plunged straight into an account of
the play's particular beauties:

> Were I to give my own opinion, I should say, that this is the
> best comedy either antient or modern, that ever was written to
> please upon the stage; for while the most superficial judges
> admire it, it is impossible but the nicest, and most accurate,
> must approve.
>
>   It is written strictly up to the rules of the drama; yet it has all
> that variety of characters and incidents, which is pleaded in
> their excuse by those who deviate from them. What fault then
> can we find in it? Oh, says somebody, it has too much Wit.
> Well, that is a fault so seldom committed, I should think we
> might overlook it for once.[5]

His response to a production of *The Way of the World* at Drury
Lane in November 1758 shows him with the same urbane and
sophisticated understanding of Congreve's qualities as a playwright:

> DRURY-LANE, *Nov.* 14. Yesterday evening at the above
> theatre was presented *The Way of the World*, a comedy,
> which for poignancy of wit; delicacy of humour; regularity of
> conduct; propriety of manners; and continuity of character; may
> (if ever work might) be reckoned a finished piece.

Mr Congreve had too intimate an acquaintance with human nature not to know that the generality of mankind have a much greater share of vices, than virtues, in their composition; and it is the business of a comic poet to turn the most glaring side outward.[6]

Essentially the same balanced view of Congreve informs the work of the actor and publisher, Thomas Davies, who in his *Memoirs of the Life of David Garrick Esq* (1780) and in his *Dramatic Miscellanies* (1784) gives an invaluable personal record of plays, players and playwrights in the Georgian theatre. In his *Dramatic Miscellanies* he provides an account of Congreve's work that is in effect a literary history in brief. His views are balanced and judicious, informed by careful analysis as well as practical experience, and his critical judgements seem completely untainted by any trace of the moral imperatives of Collier's school. Like Arthur Murphy, he generously acknowledges *Love for Love* to be one of the finest plays written in English:

By consent of all the critics, *Love for Love* is esteemed not only the most excellent of Congreve's plays, but one of the best in our language. His characters are drawn with such strength and comprehension, that his comedies are perpetual commentaries on the passions and humours of mankind. The punishment of an unnatural and hard-hearted parent is the moral aim of the poet; and in this he has, by a judicious conduct of his plot, fully succeeded.[7]

Samuel Johnson, in his *Prefaces, Biographical and Critical, to the Works of the English Poets* (completed in 1781), had turned his attention to Congreve's work just a few years before Davies published his account. He begins by acknowledging that many years have passed since he has bothered to read Congreve's plays, and then goes on to damn them with faint praise:

his characters are commonly fictitious and artificial, with very little of nature, and not much of life. He formed a peculiar idea of comick excellence, which he supposed to consist in gay remarks and unexpected answers; but that which he endeavoured, he seldom failed of performing. His scenes exhibit not

much of humour, imagery, or passion: his personages are a kind
of intellectual gladiators; every sentence is to ward or strike;
the contest of smartness is never intermitted; his wit is a meteor
playing to and fro with alternate coruscations.[8]

At one point, however, he is gripped by real enthusiasm. On the
basis of close textual analysis, he concludes that Almeria's
Temple speech from the beginning of Act 2 of *The Mourning
Bride* is one of the finest passages to be found in English poetry;
almost in the same breath Congreve's famous poem on the death
of Queen Mary he dismisses as being devoid of both wisdom and
wit.

In contrast to Thomas Davies, Johnson shows a lingering trace
of Puritan prejudice in his response to Congreve. In his account of
the Collier controversy, he allies himself firmly with the puritan
zealots:

> The cause of Congreve was not tenable: whatever glosses he
> might use for the defence or palliation of single passages, the
> general tenour and tendency of his plays must always be
> condemned. It is acknowledged, with universal conviction,
> that the perusal of his works will make no man better; and
> that their ultimate effect is to represent pleasure in alliance with
> vice, and to relax those obligations by which life ought to be
> regulated.[9]

As always in Johnson, an appeal to the common sense (all too
often the common prejudices) of his age settles the issue. If the
majority of his contemporaries find Congreve's plays morally
questionable, then clearly they are; and in Johnson's view, there is
nothing more to be said.

If Thomas Davies provides the most judicious critical introduction to Congreve's work in the eighteenth century, it is Hazlitt in
his *Lectures on the English Comic Writers* (1819) who offers
early nineteenth-century readers the most carefully balanced and
polished account of both the merits and weaknesses of Congreve
as a playwright. Of his merits he wrote with unstinting praise:

> His style is inimitable, nay perfect. It is the highest model of
> comic dialogue. Every sentence is replete with sense and satire,

conveyed in the most polished and pointed terms. Every page presents a shower of brilliant conceits, is a tissue of epigrams in prose, is a new triumph of wit, a new conquest over dulness. The fire of artful raillery is nowhere else so well kept up. [. . .] Sheridan will not bear a comparison with him in the regular antithetical construction of his sentences, and in the mechanical artifices of his style [. . .] His works are a singular treat to those who have cultivated a taste for the niceties of English style; there is a peculiar flavour in the very words, which is to be found in hardly any other writer.[10]

On the other hand, Hazlitt is perfectly capable of drawing a clear distinction, not on moral but on critical grounds, between Congreve's comedies and his one tragedy:

Our author's superiority deserted him almost entirely with his wit. His serious and tragic poetry is frigid and jejune to an unaccountable degree. His *forte* was the description of actual manners, whether elegant or absurd; and when he could not deride the one or embellish the other, his attempts at romantic passion or imaginary enthusiasm are forced, abortive, and ridiculous, or common-place. The description of the ruins of a temple in the beginning of the *Mourning Bride*, was a great stretch of his poetic genius. It has, however, been over-rated, particularly by Dr. Johnson, who could have done nearly as well himself for a single passage in the same style of moralising and sentimental description.[11]

This is genuine criticism, uncluttered by facile moral imperatives, and informed by the desire to establish the aesthetic effects, as well as the merits and defects, of Congreve's work as a dramatic poet.

It was not until the late 1880s that the first full-length account of Congreve's life and work was written. Edmund Gosse's *Life of William Congreve* (1888), while containing errors and omissions, was nevertheless a sympathetic and critically sound attempt to present Congreve's work in its historical context. It marked a genuine watershed in critical response to Congreve and his plays. For the first time, the reading public was offered a full account of Congreve's life and the issues that concerned him, including a detailed and cautiously even-handed outline of the Collier controversy. Gosse also provided invaluable information about the theatre of Congreve's day and the actors for whom he wrote. At the heart of the book, he gave thoughtful, critical introductions to the plays themselves, followed in each case by a full descriptive analysis of the action. His introduction to *Love for Love* offers a typical illustration of his approach:

> The comedy of *Love for Love* has been commonly accounted Congreve's masterpiece, and perhaps with justice. It is not quite so uniformly brilliant in style as *The Way of the World*, but it has the advantage of possessing a much wholesomer relation to humanity than that play, which is almost undiluted satire, and a more theatrical arrangement of scenes. In *Love for Love* the qualities which had shown themselves in *The Old Bachelor* and *The Double Dealer* recur, but in a much stronger degree. The sentiments are more unexpected, the language is more pictur-esque, the characters have more activity of mind and vitality of nature. All that was merely pink has deepened into scarlet; even what is disagreeable, the crudity of allusion and the indecency of phrase, – have increased. The style in all its parts and qualities has become more vivid. We are looking through the same telescope as before, but the sight is better adjusted, the outlines are more definite, and the colours more intense. So wonderfully felicitous is the phraseology that we cannot doubt that if Congreve could only have kept himself unspotted from the sins of the age, dozens of tags would have passed, like bits of Shakespeare, Pope, and Gray, into habitual parlance. In spite of its errors against decency, *Love for Love* survived on the stage for more than a century, long after the remainder of Restoration and Orange drama was well-nigh extinct.[12]

There is a clear hint of puritan disapproval towards the end of this passage, but for the most part the reader is given a lively and vivid impression of the merits of the play, based on comparisons with other Congreve plays.

Gosse's pioneering work on Congreve in 1888 paved the way for the club performances of Congreve's plays in the early years of the twentieth century. It was also the inspiration behind Montague Summers's decision to prepare the first (and still only) critical edition of Congreve's complete works, based on the original editions of Congreve's plays and poems. In a note on the text, Summers outlined the editorial principles that had guided his work:

> With regard to the plays the first quartos are scrupulously followed. Very early were considerable alterations of the text allowed. Excisions were at once made in consequence of Collier's attack. Grave corruptions, although not conceivably for reasons of prudery, almost immediately crept into the verse of *The Mourning Bride*. There is introduced a new scheme of scene division, either adapted from Molière and the French stage, or following the unusual system of Ben Jonson. In any case, whencesoever it may have been derived, this re-arrangement is wholly unsuitable for Congreve's comedies, and at several points it necessitated the writing in of fresh lines, which are awkward and abrupt. Modern editions have expunged to boot the original stage directions at will and recklessly employed a later method and design, a change entirely destructive of the theatrical technique of the plays.
>
> [Vol. 1, p. xiii]

His edition, published in 1923, was like a breath of fresh air. At last readers were offered the possibility of seeing what Congreve actually wrote, as opposed to being offered a maimed and crippled version of the original. Summers also wrote a detailed introduction on Congreve's life and work for his edition which was equally refreshing. For the first time in over 200 years, an English reading public was offered a candid and frank assessment of Collier's critical approach, and no punches were spared:

> The first thing that must strike every reader of this gallimaufry of prejudice and virulence is the absolute and portentous lack of humour which dulls and drabs each chapter. [. . .] Lambent dullness plays over the whole harangue, encrusted as it is in every part with formal and ignorant pedantry.
>
> [Vol. 1, p. 46]

In retrospect it seems quite astonishing that it took over two centuries for the voice of blunt common sense to be heard in this matter. No wonder Summers adopts a distinctly irritated posture in dismissing Collier. One's surprise is tempered by the recollection that it took just as long to lift the muzzle that was placed on the theatre in 1737 by a similar blend of political opportunism and puritan sensibility as had inspired Collier. (The Licensing Act of 1737, which imposed strict censorship on the theatre, was not finally abolished until the Theatres Act of 1968.)

Despite its importance, Montague Summers's edition was still directed at an exclusive readership. It was printed by the Nonesuch Press on expensive paper and in a limited edition. Some two years later, however, in 1925, Bonamy Dobrée published his edition of Congreve's comedies for the World's Classics Series of Oxford University Press, in a format and at a price that made the plays easily accessible. He went on to publish *The Mourning Bride, Poems and Miscellanies* in 1928 for the same series. He chose to base these two volumes on the 1710 edition of Congreve's work, arguing that the scene divisions introduced in the 1710 edition emphasised important changes in tempo, but without addressing Summers's contention that these changes were 'wholly unsuitable' and both 'awkward and abrupt'. These two volumes remained the standard edition of Congreve's plays right up to 1967 when Herbert Davis published *The Complete Plays of William Congreve*, based on the original quartos, for the University of Chicago Press.

Dobrée had already demonstrated his critical acumen in a thoughtful study and re-evaluation of Restoration Comedy, published in 1924. In this volume, entitled *Restoration Comedy, 1660–1720*, he wrote separate chapters on the major writers of the period. In respect of Congreve's work, he gave a brief résumé of Victorian critical responses to Congreve and then went on to provide his own perceptive analysis of the plays. However, his introduction to Congreve's comedies in the World's Classics edition offered, in many ways, a more illuminating and challenging account of Congreve's work. Judiciously blending close textual analysis with a historically based exposition of the way Restoration comedy had developed, Dobrée argues that the strength of Congreve's work lies specifically in its aesthetic merit:

> In discussing Congreve, then, it must be insisted that he belongs to the type of 'pure' creator, who is to be judged solely on

aesthetic grounds, that is, by the quality of delight which he imparts. He and Dickens are not to be measured by the same instrument, any more than Dostoievsky and Miss Austen, in spite of the elements they may possess in common. It is, when all is said, the province of art to delight the spirit, and it is, finally, the aesthetic pleasure we get from Congreve that earns him his high place. It is on that plane, and not on the moral or philosophic, that he has something to give.[13]

His subsequent analysis of the aesthetic strengths of *The Way of the World* is concisely and convincingly argued.

Following this spate of activity in the 1920s, it was not until 1941 that the next landmark occurred in Congreve scholarship. That year saw the publication of John Hodges's meticulously researched biography, *William Congreve the Man*. Hodges was not concerned to offer any new insights into the plays, but rather, by using fresh sources, wished to present new information about the boy and the man. In particular, he wished to clarify some of the motives for Congreve's behaviour, notably in his relationships with Anne Bracegirdle and Henrietta, Duchess of Marlborough. Although he succeeded admirably in this aim, there were still some gaps in his coverage that were filled by Kathleen Lynch in her book, *A Congreve Gallery* (1951). She too made use of manuscript source material to throw additional light on Congreve's boyhood friends as well as the people he met within the Godolphin circle. Finally, Hodges returned to his interest in Congreve many years later, publishing a scholarly edition of Congreve's letters in 1964, entitled *William Congreve: Letters and Documents*. These three volumes, based on all known source material relating to Congreve's life, provide a lucid and coherent view of Congreve the man. The gaps that remain are the direct result of Congreve's own caution and discretion in his personal affairs.

The 1950s brought some notable contributions to Congreve criticism from American New Critics. The first was Thomas Fujimara who, in his book, *The Restoration Comedy of Wit* (1952), was concerned to refute the notion that Restoration comedy in general, and Congreve in particular, were only concerned with manners, not morals. He specifically rejected Dobrée's aesthetically based interpretation of Congreve and argued instead that Congreve offered in his plays the witty presentation of a naturalistic outlook on life, which was typical of Restoration comedy as a whole, allied to something of the good sense and sensibility of the new age: 'Mrs Millamant is the perfect female Truewit, but she has developed a heart; and Mirabell is still a striking and elegant Wit, but he begins to grow sententious and sober.'[14]

At the end of the decade, Norman Holland, in his book, *The First Modern Comedies* (1959), argued with a rare blend of clarity and enthusiasm that Restoration plays (including Congreve's) are above all concerned with the conflict between manners (i.e. social conventions) and anti-social natural desires. He analysed Congreve's four comedies in great detail, concentrating in each case on the conflict in them between appearance and nature. Particularly in the case of *Love for Love*, he came to some novel and thought-provoking conclusions:

> The knowledge necessary for living in the social whirl separates Ben and Prue, who do not have it yet, from the social people who do and from Valentine and Angelica who are rising above it. Ben, Valentine, and Angelica are all seeking something outside the ordinary social framework. Ben, separated from the others by being a 'Sea-Beast', is beyond social distinctions. He refuses to come to rest, but Valentine and Angelica, by the end of the play, have gone beyond society as they wanted to.[15]

By the 1960s, Congreve criticism was turning its attention to the historical context in which Congreve lived and wrote. Combining the analytic techniques of earlier new critics with insights derived from historically based scholarship, W. H. van Voris, in his book *The Cultivated Stance: the Designs of Congreve's Plays* (1965), offered a stimulating account of the way the theme of time (and particularly the ravages of time) is built into the very structure of Congreve's plays. Even contemporary social and political ideas, as reflected in Congreve's plays, are interpreted by van Voris within this thematic framework. His conclusions on *The Way of the World* illustrate this point to good effect:

Not only the last little drama, but the whole drama of the play
would seem to be a revolutionary contrivance by Mirabell.
They have all been his actors. He has simply waited until they
said the right lines. In arranging his comedies, he has modeled
them on the comedies the Whig lords played with England in
1688. [. . .] The order that the Machiavellian Mirabell has
created now gives the World beauty and grace. Mirabell has
made his masque of order like a worldly Prospero with art that
has no magic, and his great advantage is that he can marry his
Ariel.[16]

Even more emphasis on the literary, social and political context
of Congreve's plays may be found in Maximillian Novak's book,
William Congreve (1971). This offered some sensitively argued
readings of the plays, seen in the light of contemporary literary
and social ideas. Novak's major contention was that Congreve
should be seen as an author caught between an older age of wit
and a new age of sentiment.

A quite different view of Congreve was offered by Aubrey
Williams in his book *An Approach to Congreve* (1979). Written
from a modern Christian perspective, Williams's book takes issue
both with the zealots of the Collier school and with the adherents
of a Hobbesian naturalist view of Congreve's plays. Williams
argues that far from rejecting Christian values, Congreve's plays
were written within the framework of traditionally accepted
Christian teachings, including a belief in divine providence. His
detailed analysis at times seems somewhat strained, but is at its
best in wrestling with *The Double Dealer*:

It is my own view that *The Double-Dealer*, in spite of its
Restoration *esprit* and gloss, is a genuine descendant of the
English morality play tradition [. . .]. The satanism so
insistently imputed to Maskwell by Congreve, along with a
dazzling amount of demonological allusion hitherto unnoticed
in critical discussions of the play, carries with it intimations of a
world that simply cannot be reduced to the 'naturalistic'.[17]

In addition to these historically based studies, the 1970s and
1980s have seen a series of Congreve studies based on the notion

that a proper understanding of Congreve's plays cannot be confined to a literary interpretation but must above all take account of the fact that they were written for performance.

Harold Love initiated this process with his slender monograph entitled simply *Congreve* (1974). He began his study with a succinct account of the theatre and the players for whom Congreve wrote and then went on to analyse, in each of the comedies, the way literary devices are used by Congreve to achieve specific effects in performance. In his analysis of *The Old Batchelour*, for instance, he stressed the way wit is used not merely for its own sake but as a device to show personalities in conflict. It is not simply a literary conceit but a mode of dramatic interaction. In his account of *The Way of the World* he stressed the verbal indirectness of the play. Characters not only conceal what they really think, but often state the opposite of their real feelings. Politeness, for instance, is used as a means of expressing hostility. This indirect mode of communication, which is particularly suited to the theatre, led him to argue with some vigour that in this play, 'Congreve's point of view is ultimately a moral one.'[18]

An altogether more substantial account of the importance of performance for an understanding of Restoration plays may be found in Peter Holland's book, *The Ornament of Action: Text and Performance in Restoration Comedy* (1979). The major part of the book is taken up with a very detailed examination of Restoration conventions of staging, casting, and acting, as well as the preparation of quarto play texts in conjunction with the first performance of plays. The volume concludes with an analysis of Congreve's comedies, viewed in the light of these conventions. Particularly detailed attention is paid to the way casting is used to guide an audience's response to a given character. In respect of *The Double Dealer*, for instance, Holland comments:

Mrs Barry must have raised Lady Touchwood's rantings into tragic passion. [. . .] The excess of this style is not comic but instead fractures the conventional limits of comic style. [. . .] The casting of Kynaston as Lord Touchwood should then eliminate any doubts we might entertain about the essential seriousness of the character.[19]

His detailed analysis of the plays leads him to the general conclusion that, 'The performance, the experience of the flux in the theatre, in itself becomes the end of the text.'[20] Bearing this conclusion in mind, Holland has some trenchant criticism to make of Congreve's attempt to prepare a 'reading' edition of his plays in 1710, by abandoning the original quarto texts which were intended for performance:

No one would guess from *The Works* that Congreve was a brilliant theatrical craftsman, a skilled man of the theatre. [. . .] In the search for what would constitute a reading edition, Congreve's need to elevate his drama led him to choose the wrong models.[21]

The late Jocelyn Powell's approach in his book *Restoration Theatre Production* (1984) is quite different. He begins by stressing that Restoration audiences came to the theatre, not primarily to see a play, but to experience a social occasion. It was therefore the task of both dramatists and actors to engage in a lively dialectic with this sometimes unruly audience, 'continuously riding their responses, teasing, coaxing, dominating, creating a vigorous and present dialogue between reality and imagination'.[22] Powell concludes his illuminating study of the Restoration theatre with a discerning account of *The Way of the World* in which he shows how:

One of the most important aspects of Congreve's genius as a writer for the stage is his ability to create scenes in which the moral nature of his characters is precisely defined physically as well as intellectually. He devises action to capture the essence of each character.[23]

These two volumes by Holland and Powell indicate the most recent direction taken by Congreve critics. However, the diversity of modern critical interest in Congreve is further illustrated, first, in a collection of essays edited by Brian Morris for the Mermaid Critical Commentaries Series entitled *William Congreve* (1972) and, second, in a collection of critical extracts edited by Patrick

Lyons for the Macmillan Casebook series entitled *Congreve: Comedies. A Casebook* (1982).

Finally, a compendium of critical responses to Congreve has been assembled and edited by Alexander Lindsay and Howard Erskine-Hill for Routledge's Critical Heritage Series. Entitled *William Congreve: The Critical Heritage* (1989), it presents an excellent selection of critical source material from the 1690s up to the early twentieth century. What is curious, however, is to find a modern critic in the late 1980s, *viz* Erskine-Hill in his introduction to this volume, treating Jeremy Collier's ideas with deference and respect and suggesting in all seriousness that Congreve had a 'case to answer'.[24] Clearly, the puritan tradition in English criticism dies hard.

The sheer diversity of response that Congreve's work has provoked suggests that his plays will continue to engage both the feelings and the intellect of actors, audiences and critics in future years. The challenge offered by his plays is supremely theatrical: it is to look below the glittering but confusing surface of reality to the more substantive values underneath. At a surface level, his characters on occasion may appear frivolous, cynical, self-engrossed, amoral and at times even immoral. But below the surface, they and their author are concerned with issues that matter as crucially today as then, above all with the distinction between consent and coercion in personal and political relationships and with the way individual lives and whole societies can be wrecked by appetite and ambition. Ultimately Congreve's plays are involved in the quest for what makes men and women able to live together in peace, stability and mutual respect.

The interpretation suggested by my volume is that Congreve should be seen as a profoundly political author for whom there is no distinction between public and private life. For Congreve, there can be no democratic system of government based on consent, if individual human relationships are not based on the same set of values. For him, human rights begin at home. In his plays, the worlds of micro and macro politics interlock in one set of passionately held beliefs.

The same values Congreve believed in, and explored so thoroughly in his plays, helped to build the foundations of a peacefully governed, democratic state that, throughout the eighteenth century (and for all its faults), was the envy of intellectuals all over Europe. It is my contention that those same values are as valid and necessary today in the politically changing world of the 1990s as they were in the 1690s. It is above all this that will ensure the continuing relevance and appeal of his work.

Notes

1 Life and Work

1. See A. Lindsay and H. Erskine-Hall, *William Congreve: The Critical Heritage* (London and New York: Routledge, 1989) p. 260.
2. Ibid, p. 213.
3. Ibid, p. 408.
4. Both points are illustrated in many of the letters printed in John C. Hodges (ed.), *William Congreve: Letters and Documents* (London: Macmillan, 1964).
5. Quoted from Lindsay and Erskine-Hall (1989) p. 66.
6. Quoted from John C. Hodges, *William Congreve the Man: A Biography from New Sources* (New York: Modern Language Association of America, 1941) p. 40.
7. This point was first made by Colley Cibber in his *Apology for the Life of Mr Colley Cibber, Written by Himself* [London, 1740] ed. B.R.S. Fone (Ann Arbor: University of Michigan Press, 1968) p. 98.
8. See Hodges (1941) p. 46.
9. Letter from Congreve to John Dennis, 11 August 1695. Hodges (1964) p. 188.
10. See Hodges (1941) pp. 56–7.
11. His musical setting of the text proved very popular with a modern audience in the prom concert recreation of the 1701 competition at the Royal Albert Hall, London on 13 August 1989. See Chapter 8.
12. In the 1989 recreation of the competition, the Eccles version was narrowly acclaimed as the winner but only on the casting vote of the presenter. See Chapter 8.
13. Hodges (1964) p. 21.

14. The text of the licence is reproduced in D. Thomas (ed.), *Theatre in Europe: a Documentary History*. *Restoration and Georgian England, 1660–1788* (Cambridge: Cambridge University Press, 1989) p. 22.
15. Hodges (1964) p. 35.
16. Scholars are divided in their views as to whether Congreve did in fact write his libretto for the opening of the Queen's Theatre. Stoddard Lincoln feels that this is indeed most likely. (See 'The first musical setting of Congreve's *Semele*' in *Music and Letters*, 44 (1963) pp. 105–7.) Curtis Price, on the other hand, inclines to the view that it was not ready until 1707 (see 'The Critical Decade for English Music Drama 1700–1710' in *Harvard Library Bulletin*, 26 (1978) pp. 60–1). There is no firm evidence to confirm either view. The balance of probability, however, suggests that Congreve would indeed have had his eye on the opening of the Queen's Theatre.
17. *The Complete Works of William Congreve* (Summers edn), vol. 4, p. 81.
18. See Cibber (Fone edn) p. 173.
19. See Thomas (1989) pp. 73–6.
20. Hodges (1964) p. 38.
21. See Curtis Price, 'The Critical Decade', p. 61.
22. See *A Biographical Dictionary of Actors, Actresses, Musicians, Dancers, Managers and other Stage Personnel in London. 1660–1800*, vol. 2, ed. Phillip Highfill Jr, Kalman A. Burnim and Edward Langhans (Carbondale and Edwardsville: Southern Illinois University Press, 1973) p. 276.
23. The first two verses of this poem were published by Congreve in 1710 in his collected *Poems upon Several Occasions*. The last two verses were first published from Congreve's own manuscript by Hodges (1941) p. 88.
24. From a poem by Swift entitled 'A libel on the Reverend Dr Delany and His Excellency John, Lord Carteret'. Quoted from Hodges (1941) p. 86.
25. Frances Porter was Anne Bracegirdle's sister. See Hodges (1964) p. 7.
26. See Hodges (1941) pp. 111–12.
27. Blenheim MSS. FI. 35, ff 36–7, Blenheim Palace, Woodstock, Oxon. Quoted from Kathleen M. Lynch: *A Congreve Gallery* (Cambridge, Mass: Harvard University Press, 1951) p. 75.
28. Quoted from Lynch (1951) p. 77.
29. See Lynch (1951) pp. 60–1.
30. Quoted from Lynch (1951) p. 64.

31. Hodges (1964), p. 255.
32. See Lynch (1951), p. 91.
33. Quoted from *The Mourning Bride, Poems and Miscellanies* by William Congreve, ed. Bonamy Dobrée (London: Oxford University Press, 1928) pp. 401–2.

2 The Literary Context

1. J. E. Spingarn (ed.), *Critical Essays of the Seventeenth Century*, vol. 2 (Oxford: Clarendon Press, 1908) p. 59.
2. John Dryden, *Of Dramatic Poesy and Other Critical Essays*, vol. 1, ed. George Watson (London: Dent, 1962) p. 91.
3. Ibid, p. 61.
4. See Thomas (1989), p. 190.
5. Ibid, p. 191.
6. Maurice Stone in his book *The Family, Sex and Marriage in England 1500–1800* (Harmondsworth: Penguin Books, 1979) describes the situation thus: 'in the late seventeenth century, as the concept of marriage as a sacrament ebbed with the waning of religious enthusiasm, divorce by private Act of Parliament became a possible avenue of escape for wealthy noblemen and others [. . .]. But this was a very expensive procedure, and it was almost entirely confined, especially before 1760, to those who had very large properties at stake to be handed on to a male heir by a second marriage. Between 1670 and 1799, there were only 131 such Acts, virtually all instituted by husbands, and only seventeen passed before 1750'. [p. 34]
7. Numerous passages in Pepys's diary make it clear that this was a faithful reflection of contemporary behaviour.

3 The Philosophical and Political Context

1. Thomas Hobbes, *Leviathan*, ed. C. B. Macpherson (Harmondsworth: Pelican Books, 1968) p. 161.
2. Ibid, p. 120.
3. Ibid, p. 186.
4. John Aubrey, *Brief Lives*, vol. 1, ed. Andrew Clark (Oxford: The Clarendon Press, 1898) p. 340.
5. Maurice Ashley, *England in the Seventeenth Century* (Harmondsworth: Pelican Books, 1965) p. 171.
6. Ibid, p. 178.
7. Ibid, p. 179.
8. John Locke, *Two Treatises of Government*, ed. Peter Laslett

(Cambridge: Cambridge University Press, 1967) para 87, pp. 341–2.
9. See Stone (1979) p. 136.

4 The Theatrical Context

1. *London in 1710. From the Travels of Z. C. von Uffenbach,* translated and edited by W. H. Quarrell and M. Mare (London: Faber & Faber, 1934) pp. 30–1.
2. For a detailed account of the actors' rebellion, see Judith Milhous, *Thomas Betterton and the Management of Lincoln's Inn Fields, 1695–1708* (Carbondale and Edwardsville: Southern Illinois University Press, 1979) pp. 51–74.
3. See Cibber (Fone edn) p. 111.
4. See Thomas (1989) pp. 44–6.
5. Public Record Office LC 7/3, f 22. Reproduced in Milhous (1979), pp. 249–50.
6. Cibber (Fone edn) p. 98.
7. Quoted from Thomas, (1989) p. 144.
8. John Downes, *Roscius Anglicanus or an HISTORICAL Review of the STAGE,* ed. Judith Milhous and Robert D. Hume (London: The Society for Theatre Research, 1987) p. 94.
9. Quoted from Thomas (1989) p. 73.
10. For details, see Milhous (1979) p. 192.
11. Cibber (Fone edn) p. 173.
12. For a detailed account of Vanbrugh's financial difficulties during his opera season of 1708, see Judith Milhous, 'Opera Finances in London, 1674–1738' in *Journal of the American Musicological Society,* vol. xxxvii, no 3 (1984) pp. 571–7.
13. See Chapter 8.
14. In addition to Handel, Thomas Arne was attracted to Congreve's work as a librettist and composed a new setting for his masque, *The Judgement of Paris,* which was performed at Drury Lane in March 1742. See Roger Fiske, *English Theatre Music in the Eighteenth Century* (London: Oxford University Press, 1973) p. 196.
15. Quoted from John Genest, *Some Account of the English Stage from the Restoration in 1660 to 1830,* vol. 3 (Bath, 1832) p. 389.

5 Literary Theory and Morality Debates

1. Jeremy Collier, *A Short View of the Immorality and Profaneness of the English Stage, Together With the Sense of Antiquity upon this Argument* (London: 1698) p. 1.

2. Ibid, pp. 156–7.
3. Ibid, pp. 62–3. The words in square brackets were omitted by Collier. A version of this passage is reprinted in Lindsay and Erskine-Hill (1989), p. 110.
4. Quoted from Rose Anthony, *The Jeremy Collier Stage Controversy, 1698–1726* [1937] (New York: Benjamin Blom, 1966) p. 22.
5. See Anthony (1966), p. 20.
6. A reference to Congreve's pastoral poem mourning the death of Queen Mary and to his Pindarique Ode celebrating King William's victory at Namure. See Chapter 1.
7. Quoted from Lindsay and Erskine-Hill (1989) p. 162.
8. *The Tatler* (Saturday, 16 April 1709) ed. Donald F. Bond, vol. 1 (Oxford: Clarendon Press, 1987) p. 31.
9. *The Spectator* (no 65, 15 May 1711) ed. Donald F. Bond, vol. 1 (Oxford: Clarendon Press, 1965) pp. 278–9.
10. C. Cibber, *The Dramatic Works of Colley Cibber, Esq*, vol. 2, [London, 1777] (New York: AMS Press Inc, 1966) pp. 5–6.
11. Richard Steele, *The Conscious Lovers*, in *Eighteenth Century Comedy*, ed. W.D. Taylor (London: Oxford University Press, 1929) pp. 104–5.
12. See Thomas (1989) pp. 409–19.

6 Comedies of Appetite and Contract

1. For a detailed discussion of Congreve's indebtedness to Jonson, see Brian Gibbons, 'Congreve's *The Old Batchelour* and Jonsonian Comedy' in Brian Morris (ed.) *William Congreve* (Mermaid critical commentaries) (London: Ernest Benn, 1972) pp. 3–20.
2. Dryden, op cit, p. 76.
3. See Chapter 5.
4. See Chapter 5.
5. For details of this episode, see W.H. Van Voris, *The Cultivated Stance: the Designs of Congreve's Plays* (Dublin: The Dolmen Press, 1965) p. 58.
6. The first essay is described by Locke himself as follows: 'In the former the false principles and foundation of Sir Robert Filmer and his followers are detected and overthrown.'
7. See Van Voris (1965) p. 79.
8. See H. Love, *Congreve* (Oxford: Basil Blackwell, 1974) p. 60.
9. See M.E. Novak, *William Congreve* (New York: Twayne Publishers, 1971) p. 150.

7 Tragedy, Masque and Opera

1. Jeremy Collier, *A Defence of the Short View* (London: 1698), p. 31. Reprinted in Lindsay and Erskine-Hill (1989) p. 145.
2. James Boswell, *The Life of Samuel Johnson*, vol. 1 (London: 1791) p. 317. Reprinted in Lindsay and Erskine-Hill (1989) p. 245.
3. Letter to Joseph Keally, 26 March 1701. Quoted from Hodges (1964) pp. 20–1.
4. Hodges prints a letter sent to Lord Halifax by George Stepney, Envoy To Vienna, where this emerges. See Hodges (1964) p. 21, note 4.
5. Handel's musical treatment of this scene, in his 1744 version, makes this quite clear.
6. See the *Dictionary of National Biography*, vol. 6.
7. See Chapter 1.

8 Congreve in Production

1. The details are given in Emmett L. Avery, *Congreve's Plays on the Eighteenth-century Stage* (New York: Modern Language Association of America, 1951) p. 75.
2. See Avery (1951) pp. 55, 75, 120.
3. See Thomas (1989) p. 157.
4. See Avery (1951) p. 74.
5. Ibid, p. 75.
6. Francis Gentleman, *The Dramatic Censor, or Critical Companion*, vol. 2 (London: J.Bell, 1770) p. 417. Reprinted in Lindsay and Erskine-Hill (1989) p. 249.
7. Ibid, p. 414. Reprinted in Lindsay and Erskine-Hill, (1989) p. 247.
8. Tate Wilkinson, *Memoirs of His Own Life by Tate Wilkinson, Patentee of the Theatres Royal, York and Hull*, vol. 1 (Dublin: Byrne, Wogan *et al.*, 1791) p. 34.
9. See Avery (1951) p. 95.
10. See Anon: *The Life of Mrs Abington* (London: Reader, 1888) p. 35.
11. Thomas Davies, *Memoirs of the Life of David Garrick*, vol. 2, (London: Thomas Davies, 1780) pp. 170–1.
12. See *The Life of Mrs Abington*, p. 87.
13. Davies (1780) vol. 2, pp. 170–1.
14. Reprinted in Avery (1951) p. 126 and Lindsay and Erskine-Hill (1989) p. 256.
15. See Thomas (1989) p. 220.

16. Davies (1780), vol. 1, pp. 190–1.
17. Quoted from Avery (1951) p. 138.
18. Ibid and Lindsay and Erskine-Hill (1989) p. 294.
19. Reprinted in Avery (1951) p. 152 and Lindsay and Erskine-Hill (1989) p. 301.
20. Nigel Playfair, *The Story of the Lyric Theatre, Hammersmith* [London, 1925] (New York: Benjamin Blom, 1969) p. 184. Reprinted in Patrick Lyons (ed.) *Congreve: Comedies. A Casebook* (London: Macmillan, 1982) p. 230.
21. Reprinted in James Agate, *The Contemporary Theatre* (London, 1924) p. 303, and Lyons (1982) p. 228.
22. John Gielgud, *Stage Directions* (London: Heinemann, 1963) p. 64.
23. Quoted from Kenneth Muir 'Congreve on the Modern Stage' in Brian Morris (ed.): *William Congreve* [Mermaid critical commentaries] (London: Ernest Benn, 1972) p. 146.
24. Ibid, p. 145.
25. Gielgud, p. 67. Reprinted in Lyons (1982) p. 231.
26. Quoted from Muir (1972) p. 149.
27. Reprinted in Lyons (1982) pp. 233–4.
28. See Muir (1972) pp. 144–5 for extracts from press reviews.
29. Ibid, p. 143.
30. For a detailed analysis of the acting style of Betterton and Barry, based on contemporary documents, see Thomas (1989) pp. 143–9.

9 Critical Responses

1. John Dryden, 'To my dear friend Mr Congreve, on his comedy, call'd, *The Double-Dealer*' in *The Double Dealer* (London: 1694). Reprinted in Lindsay and Erskine-Hill (1989) pp. 82–3.
2. See Chapter 5 for detailed quotations from Collier's *Short View*.
3. Thomas Babington Macaulay, 'Comic Dramatists of the Restoration' in *The Edinburgh Review* (1841) 72, pp. 490–528. Reprinted in Lindsay and Erskine-Hill (1989) pp. 373 and 375.
4. Richard Blackmore, *King Arthur: An Heroic Poem* (London, 1697). Reprinted in Lindsay and Erskine-Hill (1989) p. 103.
5. *The London Chronicle, or, Universal Evening Post*, 12–14 October 1758. Reprinted in Lindsay and Erskine-Hill (1989) p. 233.
6. *The London Chronicle, or, Universal Evening Post*, 14–16 November 1758. Reprinted in Lindsay and Erskine-Hill (1989) p. 234.
7. Thomas Davies, *Dramatic Miscellanies*, vol. 3 (London: Thomas Davies, 1783–4) p. 327. Reprinted in Lindsay and Erskine-Hill (1989), p. 278.

8. Samuel Johnson, *Prefaces, Biographical and Critical, to the Works of the English Poets*, vol. 6 (London, 1779–81) pp. 1–38. Reprinted in Lindsay and Erskine-Hill (1989), p. 267.
9. Ibid. Reprinted in Lindsay and Erskine-Hill (1989) p. 264.
10. William Hazlitt, *Lectures on the English Comic Writers* (London, 1819) pp. 135–46. Reprinted in Lindsay and Erskine-Hill (1989) pp. 313–14.
11. Hazlitt. Reprinted in Lindsay and Erskine-Hill (1989), pp. 317–18.
12. Edmund Gosse, *Life of William Congreve* (London: Walter Scott, 1888) pp. 69–70. Other selections from Gosse's *Life* are reprinted in Lindsay and Erskine-Hill (1989) pp. 411–19.
13. Op cit, pp. xvi–xvi.
14. Thomas H. Fujimura, *The Restoration Comedy of Wit* (Princeton University Press, 1952) p. 195.
15. Norman H. Holland, *The First Modern Comedies: The Significance of Etherege, Wycherley and Congreve* (Harvard University Press, 1959) p. 171.
16. W. H. van Voris, *The Cultivated Stance: The Designs of Congreve's Plays* (Dublin: The Dolmen Press, 1965) pp. 149–151.
17. Aubrey L. Williams, *An Approach to Congreve* (New Haven and London: Yale University Press, 1979) p. 131.
18. Harold Love, *Congreve* (Oxford: Blackwell, 1974) p. 100.
19. Peter Holland, *The Ornament of Action. Text and Performance in Restoration comedy* (Cambridge: Cambridge University Press, 1979), pp. 218–19.
20. Ibid, p. 243.
21. Ibid, p. 137.
22. Jocelyn Powell, *Restoration Theatre Production* (London: Routlege & Kegan Paul, 1984) p. 22.
23. Ibid, p. 182.
24. Lindsay and Erskine-Hill (1989) p. 20.

Select Bibliography

1 COLLECTED EDITIONS OF CONGREVE'S PLAYS

The Complete Works of William Congreve, ed. Montague Summers, 4 vols (London: The Nonesuch Press, 1923).
The Comedies of Congreve, ed. Bonamy Dobrée [The World's Classics] (London: Oxford University Press, 1925).
The Mourning Bride, Poems and Miscellanies, ed. Bonamy Dobrée [The World's Classics] (London: Oxford University Press, 1928).
The Complete Plays of William Congreve, ed. Herbert Davis (Chicago and London: University of Chicago Press, 1967).

2 BIOGRAPHICAL STUDIES

Gosse, Edmund, *Life of William Congreve* (London: Walter Scott, 1888).
Hodges, John C., *William Congreve the Man: A Biography from New Sources* (New York: Modern Language Association of America, 1941).
Hodges, John C., (ed.): *William Congreve: Letters and Documents* (London: Macmillan, 1964).
Lynch, Kathleen M: *A Congreve Gallery* (Cambridge Mass: Harvard University Press, 1951).

3 THE SOCIAL AND POLITICAL BACKGROUND

Ashley, Maurice: *England in the Seventeenth Century* (Harmondsworth: Pelican Books, 1965).

Aubrey, John: *Brief Lives*, ed. Andrew Clark (Oxford: The Clarendon Press, 1898) 2 vols.

Fraser, Antonia, *The Weaker Vessel: Woman's Lot in Seventeenth-century England* (London: Weidenfeld & Nicolson, 1984).

Hill, Christopher, *The Century of Revolution, 1602–1714* (London: Nelson, 1961).

Hobbes, Thomas, *Leviathan*, ed. C. B. Macpherson (Harmondsworth: Pelican Books, 1968).

Locke, John, *Two Treatises of Government*, ed. Peter Laslett (Cambridge: Cambridge University Press, 1967).

Loftis, John, *Comedy and Society from Congreve to Fielding* (Stanford: Stanford University Press, 1959).

Malekin, Peter, *Liberty and Love: English Literature and Society, 1640–88* (London: Hutchinson, 1981).

Ogg, David, *England in the Reigns of James II and William III* (London: Oxford University Press, 1955).

Plumb, J. H., *England in the Eighteenth Century* (Harmondsworth: Pelican Books, 1950).

Stone, Maurice, *The Family, Sex and Marriage in England, 1500–1800* (Harmondsworth: Penguin Books, 1979).

Trevelyan, G. M., *England under the Stuarts* (London: Methuen, 1904).

Willey, Basil, *The seventeenth-century background* (Harmondsworth: Peregrine Books, 1962).

4 THEATRE HISTORY: SOURCES AND STUDIES

Anon., *The Life of Mrs Abington* (London: Reader, 1888).

Anthony, Sister Rose, *The Jeremy Collier Stage Controversy, 1698–1726* [1937] (New York: Benjamin Blom, 1966).

Avery, Emmett L., *Congreve's Plays on the Eighteenth-century Stage* (New York: Modern Language Association of America, 1951).

Cibber, Colley, *An Apology for the Life of Colley Cibber: with an Historical View of the Stage during His Own Time Written by Himself*. ed. B.R.S. Fone (Ann Arbor: University of Michigan Press, 1968).

Craik, T. W. (ed), *The Revels History of Drama in English, 1660–1750*, (London: Methuen, 1976) vol. 5.

Davies, Thomas, *Memoirs of the Life of David Garrick Esq*, (London: Thomas Davies, 1780) 2 vols.

Davies, Thomas, *Dramatic Miscellanies*, (London: Thomas Davies, 1784) 3 vols.

Downes, John, *Roscius Anglicanus, or An Historical Review of the Stage* [1708], ed. J. Milhous and R. D. Hume (London: Society for Theatre Research, 1987).

Fiske, Roger, *English Theatre Music in the Eighteenth Century* (London: Oxford University Press, 1973).

Freeman, Arthur (ed.) *The English Stage: Attack and Defense, 1570–1730* (New York and London: Garland, 1973) 50 vols [facsimile reproductions of original works].

Genest, John, *Some Account of the English Stage from the Restoration in 1660 to 1830* (Bath: Carrington, 1832) 10 vols.

Gentleman, Francis, *The Dramatic Censor, or Critical Companion,* (London: J. Bell, 1770) 2 vols.

Gray, Charles H., *Theatrical Criticism in London to 1795* (New York: Columbia University Press, 1931).

Hume, Robert D. (ed.): *The London Theatre World, 1660–1800* (Carbondale & Edwardsville: Southern Illinois University Press, 1980).

Krutch, J. W., *Comedy and Conscience after the Restoration* [1924] (New York: Columbia University Press, 1961).

Leacroft, Richard, *The Development of the English Playhouse* (London: Eyre Methuen, 1973).

Lincoln, Stoddard, 'The First Musical Setting of Congreve's Semele' in *Music and Letters*, 44 (1963) pp. 103–17.

Milhous, Judith, *Thomas Betterton and the Management of Lincoln's Inn Fields, 1695–1708* (Carbondale and Edwardsville: Southern Illinois University Press, 1979).

Mullin, Donald C., *The Development of the Playhouse* (Berkeley: University of California Press, 1970).

Price, Curtis A., 'The Critical Decade for English Music Drama 1700–1710' in *Harvard Library Bulletin*, 26 (1978) pp. 38–76.

Russell, Clark W., *Representative Actors* (London: Frederick Warne, 1883).

Thomas, David (ed.) *Theatre in Europe: A Documentary History. Restoration and Georgian England, 1660–1788* (Cambridge: Cambridge University Press, 1989).

5 CRITICAL ANALYSIS OF PLAYS AND PERFORMANCE

Dobrée, Bonamy, *Restoration Comedy, 1660–1720* (London: Oxford University Press, 1924).

Fujimara, Thomas H., *The Restoration Comedy of Wit* (Princeton: Princeton University Press, 1952).

Holland, Norman H., *The First Modern Comedies* (Cambridge Mass: Harvard University Press, 1959).

Holland, Peter, *The Ornament of Action: Text and Performance in Restoration Comedy* (Cambridge: Cambridge University Press, 1979).

Hume, Robert D., *The Development of English Drama in the Late Seventeenth Century* (Oxford: Clarendon Press, 1976).

Love, Harold., *Congreve* (Oxford: Basil Blackwell, 1974).

Novak, Maximillian E., *William Congreve* (New York: Twayne Publishers, 1971).

Powell, Jocelyn, *Restoration Theatre Production* (London: Routledge & Kegan Paul, 1984).

Rothstein, Eric, *Restoration Tragedy* (Madison: University of Wisconsin Press, 1967).

Van Voris, W. H: *The Cultivated Stance: the Designs of Congreve's Plays* (Dublin: The Dolmen Press, 1965).

Williams, Aubrey L., *An Approach to Congreve* (New Haven & London: Yale University Press, 1979).

6 COLLECTIONS OF ESSAYS

Lindsay, Alexander and Erskine-Hill, Howard (eds) *William Congreve: The Critical Heritage* (London & New York: Routledge, 1989).

Lyons, Patrick (ed.) *Congreve: Comedies. A Casebook* [Macmillan Casebook] (London: Macmillan, 1982).

Morris, Brian (ed.) *William Congreve* [Mermaid Critical Commentaries] (London: Ernest Benn, 1972).

Russell Brown, John (ed.) *Restoration Theatre* [Stratford-upon-Avon Studies 6] (London: Edward Arnold, 1965).

Spingarn, J. E. (ed.) *Critical Essays of the Seventeenth Century* (Oxford: Clarendon Press, 1908) 3 vols.

Index

174